Windows 95

Quick & Easy

Windows® 95

Quick & Easy

Second Edition

Robert Cowart

SYBEX®

San Francisco • Paris • Düsseldorf • Soest

ACQUISITIONS MANAGER: *Kristine Plachy*
DEVELOPMENTAL EDITOR: *Richard Mills*
EDITOR: *Valerie Potter*
TECHNICAL EDITOR: *Maurie Duggan*
BOOK DESIGNER: *Helen Bruno; modified by Dina F Quan*
DESKTOP PUBLISHER: *Dina F Quan*
PRODUCTION COORDINATOR: *Sarah Lemas*
INDEXER: *Ted Laux*
COVER DESIGNER: *Design Site*
COVER PHOTOGRAPHER: *Mark Johann*

Library of Congress Card Number: 95-69863
ISBN: 0-7821-1511-X

Manufactured in the United States of America
10 9 8 7 6 5 4 3 2 1

To Kirsten for her unswerving friendship

Acknowledgments

First, I'd like to thank Christian Crumlish for preparing this edition. I'm also grateful to Richard Mills for his thorough and insightful help with the development of this edition. Thanks to Val Potter, my editor, who tightened up the manuscript and the figures quite nicely and showed great patience throughout the course of the project. Maurie Duggan subjected the book to a demanding technical edit, ensuring the accuracy, and more important, the clarity of the explanations.

Thanks also to Sarah Lemas, the production coordinator, and Dina Quan, the desktop publisher, who also played a major role in designing the book, based on Helen Bruno's original design. And thanks to Ted Laux, the consummate indexer.

Contents at a Glance

ix

Contents

Contents

Part Two: Just Press Start to Do Anything

LESSON **4**

STARTING A PROGRAM   **22**

LESSON **5**

SWITCHING TO A DIFFERENT TASK   **29**

LESSON **6**

REOPENING A DOCUMENT   **35**

Introduction

Computers are supposed to make life easier. But let's face it—ten years ago, all you needed to write a letter was a typewriter and a bottle of white-out. Nowadays it seems you need a degree in computer science and a training class in WordPerfect.

But things are getting better. You may have heard that Windows 95 takes much of the guesswork and pain out of using your PC. This is definitely true. Still, you have to get familiar with Windows, and, even as a veteran computer user, I was confused a bit at first.

What Makes This Book Quick & Easy?

As you probably know, a ton of information about Windows 95 comes flooding at you from all directions, all the time. Everyone from book publishers to seminar promoters is rushing to cash in on the Windows phenomenon. With new Windows titles appearing daily on bookstore shelves, it's no surprise that buyers get confused about which one to purchase. Some of these books are quite hefty tomes. (For example, I've written another book about Windows, *Mastering Windows 95* (Sybex, 1995), which is well over 1,000 pages long!)

Not everyone wants to know *everything* about Windows. Some people want just enough information to get around. A huge book might end up sitting on your shelves—just another reason not to learn to use your computer! If all you want to do is write letters, send e-mail, or set up simple spreadsheets, this book is for you.

With *Windows 95 Quick & Easy*, you don't have to be a computer jock, or even comfortable with computers, to follow the instructions. I'll lead you through all the basics of Windows in about 200 pages. You'll be up and running with Windows 95 in no

ion

time. I've written it based on my experience with people who are either afraid of computers, or completely inexperienced, so I've been particularly careful to leave out the computer gobbledegook that could bog you down. I've made every effort to tell you only what you need to know to learn to use Windows 95 quickly—sparing you the boring or nonessential.

I've written most of the book in step-by-step instructions side by side with clear full-color pictures to make following along even easier. The pictures show exactly what you should expect to see on the screen and the words tell you exactly what you're supposed to do. You can actually learn almost all you need to know just by looking at the pictures. (There are rare circumstances in which what I show on my screen and what you see on yours may differ. When that occurs, I'll give you plenty of warning so you won't feel cast adrift.) Sprinkled throughout are notes offering hints, context, further explanation, and warnings.

The book is broken down into 30 bite-sized lessons. At the beginning of each lesson is an estimated time, so you'll have an idea how long each one will take. It's not a race! No one's holding a timer over you. The clocks are there just to help you budget your time.

Naturally, Windows 95 comes with a manual, as do other software products. But out of necessity manuals tell you *everything* about a program, and they are organized as reference books rather than learning aids. Often they're written in technobabble instead of plain English.

By the time you're done reading this book, you'll be completely comfortable working with Windows. You'll know how to start programs, how to find documents, how to organize your work, and even how to send e-mail and browse the Internet.

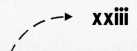

Before We Get Going

The lessons and steps in this book are designed to teach you Windows 95 in an order that makes sense. Though you may be tempted to skip around between lessons, my advice is to do them in order. That way, new terms or concepts that I build on will make sense, and you'll have the reassurance of your screen matching what you see in the pictures on the page.

There are bound to be some slight differences, nevertheless, between what you see on your screen and what's shown in the book, because of the differences between types of computers, or because someone else may have used your computer and adjusted Windows a bit already. I've tried to write the examples and instructions to prevent this from happening. If your screen looks seriously different from the illustrations in the book, have someone who knows about Windows 95 try to get you back to square one.

With that said, move on to Lesson 1 and start learning how easy Windows can make your PC.

PART ONE

Discovering the Windows 95 Desktop

Yes, Windows 95 can be quite easy to use, but right now it's still exotic, strange, and unfamiliar. In this part you'll take a look around the Desktop, poke and prod a few icons, and get used to moving and positioning open windows.

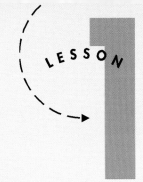

5 MINUTES

Getting Started

Sitting down in front of a computer can be scary. No matter how many advances have come about to make the machine more friendly or easy to use, it's natural for you to feel some trepidation. Sure, Windows 95 is more functional *and* attractive, by leaps and bounds, than earlier versions of Windows; still, it's yet another system for you to learn and become comfortable with.

> **NOTE**
> What is Windows, anyway? That's a good question. Windows is what the techie types call an *operating system*. It controls your computer and all of your communication with it. When you type something or click your mouse, Windows tells the computer what you're trying to do. Windows also establishes the look and feel of your computer screen. It makes programs all look about the same (as we'll soon see). It makes them all work more or less the same way too. Most people use Windows in two ways: to start programs and to organize information on the computer's hard disk.

You Won't Break Anything

Nothing bad is going to happen. To get started with Windows 95 you're going to have to plunge in and start telling your computer what to do. That means, to begin with, that you have to turn your computer on. Sounds obvious, I know, but it bears mentioning. Each computer is physically different, but the on/off switch is probably somewhere on the front of the unit with the disk slots.

- Push the power button.

- Depending on your computer, you might also need to turn on the monitor (screen) and extra units, such as speakers.

Windows 95 will take a minute or two to get everything going and then will display its Desktop and Welcome dialog box:

The Welcome dialog box comes up every time you start Windows, until you uncheck this box.

NOTE

You might first be presented with a dialog box asking for your password. If you don't want or need a password, just leave it blank and click OK. If you share your computer with other people, you may each have a different name and password. Also, if this is the very first time you or anyone else has run this version of Windows 95, some other steps will occur. For help following those one-time-only steps, see Appendix A.

3

Don't Be Afraid to Point and Click

Here's your first opportunity to tell the computer to do something. With mouse in hand, direct the pointer to the bottom-right corner of the Welcome dialog box and click the Close button. This reveals the Windows Desktop in all its glory:

The backdrop pattern, or wallpaper, will almost certainly be something other than this Egyptian design.

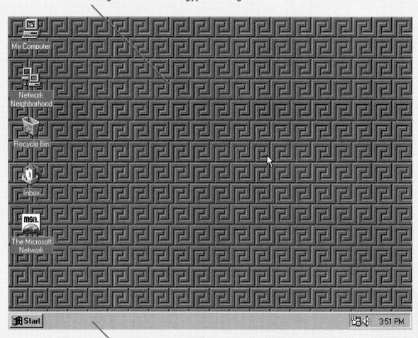

The Taskbar gives you total control over the program or programs you're running at any time.

The Desktop has a bunch of icons and other elements on it:

- *My Computer* gives you direct access to anything stored on your computer.

- You'll only have a *Network Neighborhood* icon if your computer is connected to a network.

- Anything deleted, erased, or thrown away will go to the *Recycle Bin*. Until you empty it, deleted things are still easily retrievable.

- You may or may not have an *Inbox* depending on how Windows was set up on your computer.

- Likewise, you may or may not have a *Microsoft Network* icon.

- You may have other icons lined up here as well, such as *My Briefcase*. Don't worry if things look a little different for you.

- The *Start button* on the *Taskbar* can be used to begin just about anything you'll ever want to do with your computer.

There, that wasn't so bad, was it? Now just about anything you might want to accomplish will most likely involve that same maneuver—aiming the mouse pointer at something and clicking.

5 MINUTES

Clicking, Double-Clicking, and Right-Clicking

So far you've barely had a chance to do anything. We'll soon fix that.

Single-Clicking

Generally, when you want to select something on the Windows screen, you click on it with the left button of your mouse pointer. Try this now.

1 Click the My Computer icon to select it.

> **NOTE**
>
> *Selecting* something on the computer screen means putting the focus on it before doing something to it. For a lot of commands, your computer first needs to know exactly what the object of the command is. Selected objects will change appearance, usually becoming darker or highlighted.

But selecting things is only half the fun.

Double-Clicking

If you want to *open up* or *start* something, you usually have to *double-click*, which means to click twice in a row very quickly.

● Double-click the My Computer icon to open it.

Each window's title bar has a Minimize button, a Maximize button, and a Close button.

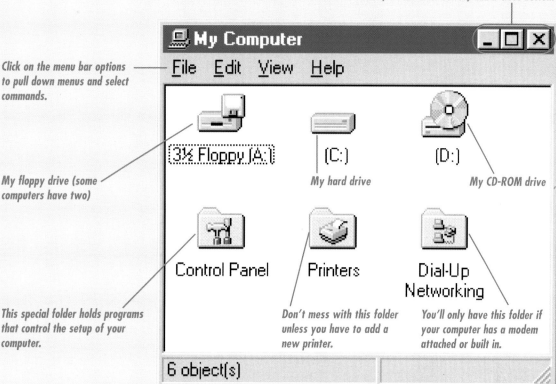

Click on the menu bar options to pull down menus and select commands.

My floppy drive (some computers have two)

My hard drive

My CD-ROM drive

This special folder holds programs that control the setup of your computer.

Don't mess with this folder unless you have to add a new printer.

You'll only have this folder if your computer has a modem attached or built in.

2 Back to single-clicking, click the *Close button* in the upper-right corner of the My Computer window.

Right-Clicking

There's one other mouse trick you'll need to know about: clicking the *right* mouse button. Throughout Windows 95, aiming the pointer at an object (or even the Desktop) and clicking the right mouse button will bring up a specialized menu of useful options.

7

For example, try this:

1   Position the mouse pointer over the My Computer icon again and click the *right* mouse button. A menu pops up. (You don't need to know yet what all these menu options do.)

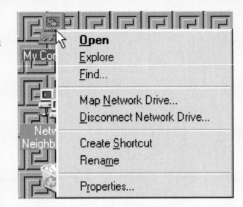

2   Click anywhere else to make the menu disappear.

3   Now position the mouse pointer over the Recycle Bin icon and click the right mouse button.

▶   A slightly different menu pops up. Notice the Empty Recycle Bin option, one of the more likely tasks you might want to perform on the Recycle Bin.

4   Again, click anywhere to make the menu disappear.

5   Finally, position the mouse pointer over the empty Desktop space and click the right mouse button. Yet another menu pops up.

6 Click somewhere else to make the menu disappear.

Now you have the basic skills you need to do anything with Windows.

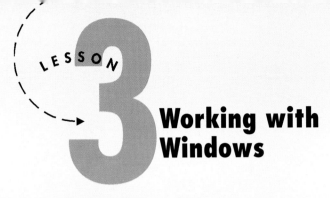

Working with Windows

As you discovered in Lesson 2, you can double-click an icon to open it or run the program it represents. When you do this, a window appears on the Desktop. Often you'll have more than one window open at a time. You can have open Desktop windows (such as My Computer and others), programs running inside their own windows, even several windows open for a single program.

You might as well start getting used to handling windows now. Let's get some windows open on the screen so you can play around with them.

Opening Windows

Start off by opening My Computer, just as you did in Lesson 2.

1 Double-click the My Computer icon.

2 In the My Computer window that appears, double-click the (C:) hard drive icon.

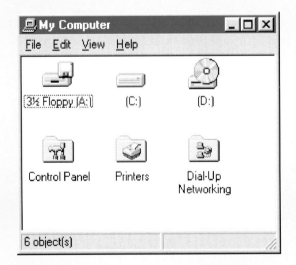

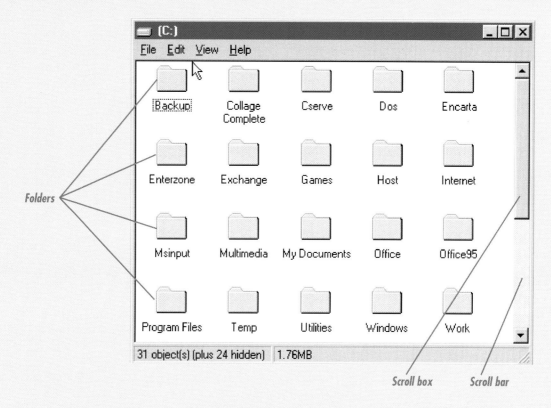

Folders

Scroll box   Scroll bar

Another window opens, showing the contents of the hard drive. (There's no special reason why the contents of your hard drive should match mine.)

- *Folders* can contain files (programs and documents) and other folders.

- If a window's contents can't all fit comfortably, a *scroll bar* allows you to scroll the view.

- The size of the *scroll box*, compared to the size of the full scroll bar, shows what portion of the window's contents are visible.

3 If the Windows folder is not visible in the window, click the scroll box and, holding down the mouse button, drag it down the scroll bar until the Windows folder comes into view.

4 Now double-click the Windows folder.

There. Now we've got a few different windows open. Notice that there's a button on the Taskbar for each window open on the Desktop. We'll get to the Taskbar soon.

NOTE

The folders and program icons shown in the Windows window appear in a different style from those in the other windows. Although they are preset this way, you can change the way the contents of any Desktop windows are displayed. But let's not get into that right now—we'll cover that in Lesson 16.

Hiding and Closing Windows

Now the screen's getting kind of cluttered, isn't it? Let's clean it up a little bit. You have two choices: You can *minimize* a window but keep it available (on the Taskbar), or you can *close* it outright.

Minimizing a Window

Try hiding the Windows window now:

1 Click the Minimize button in the title bar of the Windows window.

▶ The window shrinks down to its button on the Taskbar.

2 To bring the window back up onto the screen, just click its button on the Taskbar.

> **NOTE**
>
> You may want to neaten the windows on your screen without actually minimizing them. You can automatically arrange your windows into an orderly *cascade* of windows, each one a little down and to the right of the one below, or into *tiles* that cover the whole screen, dividing it evenly. We'll get to that in Lesson 5.

Closing a Window

If you're finished with a window, you can close it rather than minimizing it. Then it won't shrink to the Taskbar but will simply disappear from the screen.

> **NOTE**
>
> If you close a program window, you'll be exiting the program, and you'll be asked to save any unsaved work you've done. We'll get to that in the next lesson.

Try closing the Windows window now.

1 Click the Close button in the upper-right corner of the Windows window.

▶ The window closes and its button disappears from the Taskbar.

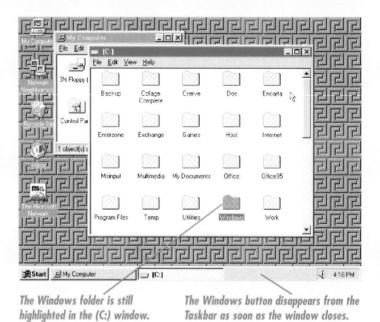

The Windows folder is still highlighted in the (C:) window.

The Windows button disappears from the Taskbar as soon as the window closes.

If you double-click a folder inside a Desktop window, the window that opens is called a *child* of the original window, which is called the *parent*. At any time, you can close a window, and its parent, and its parent's parent, and so on, just by holding down the Shift key when you click the Close button on the child window.

Let's open up a few more windows and demonstrate:

2 Double-click the Windows folder again to reopen the Windows window.

3 Double-click the System folder in the Windows window.

4 In the System window, double-click the Color folder.

5 Now hold down the Shift key and click the Close button in the upper-right corner of the Color window.

▶ All the open windows close.

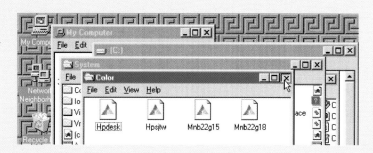

Changing the Size, Shape, or Location of a Window

There are a few more things you'll need to know how to do to windows, so we need to get one back open on the screen:

1 Once again, double-click the My Computer icon to open the My Computer window.

Maximizing a Window

Yes, it's wonderful that Windows allows you to have 20 programs running at once and all that, but the fact is, like most people, you'll usually have one main thing you're working on at a time. To focus on a single task, you can maximize a window so it takes over the whole screen (except for the Taskbar).

2 Click the Maximize button on the My Computer title bar.

15

▶ It expands to take over the whole screen (nearly). Notice now that the Maximize button has changed into something else, namely the Restore button. The Restore button takes a maximized window and returns it to the size and shape it had before it was maximized.

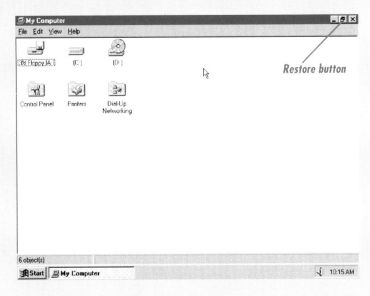

Restore button

3 Click the Restore button.

The My Computer window returns to its original size and shape.

> **NOTE**
>
> There's a shortcut for maximizing or restoring a window: double-clicking the title bar. Try it now with the My Computer window. Double-click the title bar once to maximize the window and then double-click the title bar again to restore the window.

Resizing a Window

But you're not stuck with just the window's original size or the piggy take-over-the-whole-screen size. You can resize a window any time you want to any size you want. If you move the mouse pointer over the edge or corner of a window, it will change to a resizing pointer.

1 Move the mouse pointer to the lower-right corner of the My Computer window.

2 Try this with the other three corners of the window. The pointer changes each time.

3 Now move the pointer to the right edge of the window.

4 Try this with the other three sides of the window.

5 Now click the lower-right corner of the window and drag it down and to the right.

▶ The window grows to the new size. Your icons and folders may rearrange themselves to fit the new size.

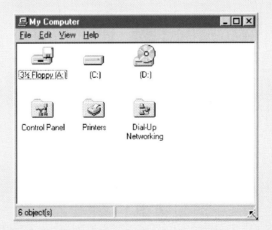

Moving a Window

Moving a window couldn't be easier. You just click the title bar and drag the window to a new position.

1 Click the title bar of the My Computer window and drag its ghost frame down and to the right.

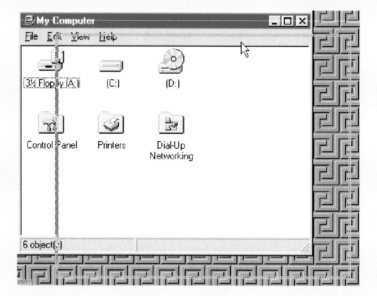

▶ As soon as you release the mouse button, the window jumps to where you moved its frame.

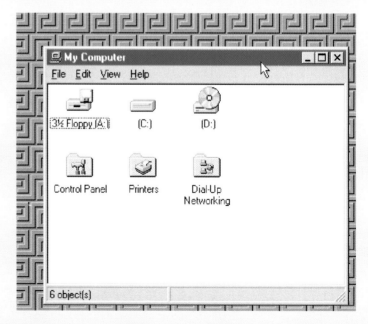

2 Click the Close button to close the My Computer window.

NOTE

If you close a window after resizing or moving it, and then reopen it at another time, it will appear in the last place you moved it to, in the size you gave it.

Now you know all you need to know about windows. It's time to really Start.

PART TWO

Just Press Start to Do Anything

Just about everything you'll ever want to do with your computer is available to you on the Start menu. By pressing the Start button you can start up a program, open a document you worked on recently, change the setup of your computer, get help, and even shut down the whole shebang.

The Start button lives on the Taskbar, which gives you complete and easy control over every program you're running. This part takes you on a test drive of the Start button and familiarizes you with the Taskbar.

4 Starting a Program

5 MINUTES

The easiest way to do almost anything in Windows 95 is to click the *Start button*. With the Start button you can run programs, reopen documents you worked on recently, change the setup of your computer, look for missing files, get help, and shut down your computer.

The most common of these activities is starting a program. Sure, Windows looks pretty, but the whole point of having a computer is to get work done (or have some fun) with it, and that always involves running a program.

Just Click Start

Windows comes with a number of useful little programs—sometimes called *accessories* and sometimes *applets*, depending on whom you ask. Since I can be sure that you have these programs, we'll use them in the steps ahead.

1 Click the Start button. The *Start menu* pops up.

Here's what each of the options is for:

- *Programs* brings up a submenu of programs or folders containing programs (the little arrowhead tells you there's a submenu lurking here).

- The *Documents* submenu gives you easy access to whatever documents you worked on most recently.

- The *Settings* submenu lets you change the setup of your computer, fiddle with printers, or customize the Taskbar itself.

- The *Find* submenu helps you look for missing files and other things.

- The *Help* command brings up Windows Help.

- The *Run* command is a throwback to the old days, when you had to type in the location and name of a file that you wanted to run.

- You click *Shut Down* when you're ready to turn off your computer.

Running a Program

2 Move the pointer to the Programs option (at the top of the Start menu) to bring up the Programs submenu. (Menu options with folders and arrowheads open up sub-submenus.)

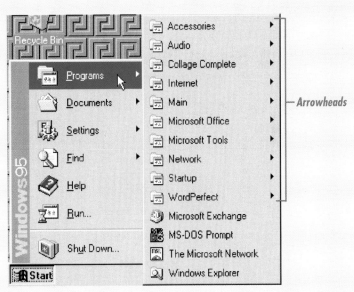

— *Arrowheads*

> **NOTE**
> Your Programs submenu will almost certainly differ from mine. The programs and folders that appear on it will depend on how your computer is set up and whether or not it had Windows 3.1 installed on it before Windows 95 came around.

3 Move the pointer to the Accessories folder option (at or near the top of the Programs submenu). Your sub-submenu might have some different items on it—don't let this bother you.

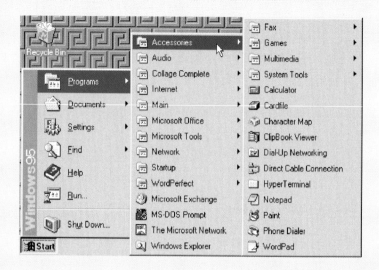

4 Click the Notepad option in the Accessories sub-submenu.

▶ This starts the Notepad program in a new window.

It says Untitled here because you haven't saved anything yet.

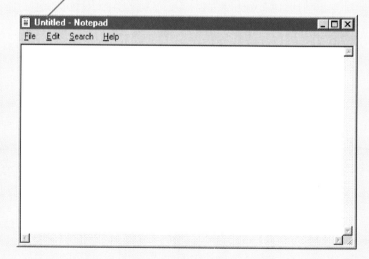

NOTE

If the program you want to run is not on the Start menu or its submenus, you can add it easily (see Lesson 7). Different programs might be there depending on whether your computer came with Windows 95 installed or had an earlier version of Windows (such as 3.1) on it. Any Windows 3.1 program group becomes an option with a sub-submenu on the Programs submenu. Likewise, any accessories in a Windows 3.1 Accessories group will appear in the Accessories sub-submenu.

Making a Document

Notepad is a simple writing program—a text editor. It has many fewer features than a word processor, but it's useful for jotting down notes (hence its name) and for short, unformatted documents.

1 Type This is my first Windows 95 document.

2 Click the File menu in the upper-left of the Notepad window (under the title bar).

▶ A menu pops up.

3 Select Save from the menu.

NOTE

I'll explain all about saving and other things you do with documents later. For now, just trust me and follow the steps.

▶ This brings up the Save As dialog box.

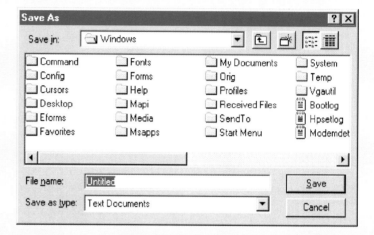

4 Type **My first document** (it will show up in the *File name* box) and press ↵.

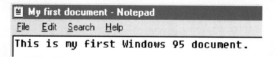

▶ The Notepad title bar now reflects the new document name.

Starting Another Program

Now, let's get a couple more programs started. I'm going to run all the submenus together this time.

1 Click Start ➤ Programs ➤ Accessories ➤ Paint, as shown.

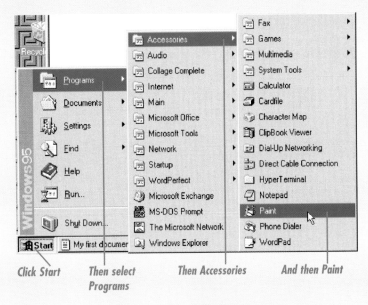

Click Start   *Then select Programs*   *Then Accessories*   *And then Paint*

▶ This brings up Paint, a simple picture-making program.

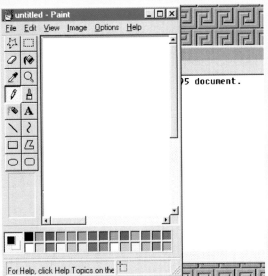

Let's start one more accessory.

2 Click Start ➤ Programs ➤ Accessories ➤ WordPad.

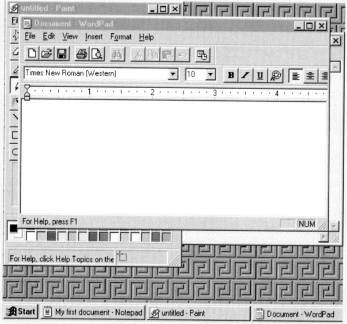

▶ This brings up WordPad, a simple word-processing program given away with Windows 95. Though not as powerful as such commercial programs as WordPerfect and Microsoft Word, it's nonetheless a fairly full-featured program. (Notice how each program gets a button in the Taskbar.)

See how easy it is to start programs with the Start button?

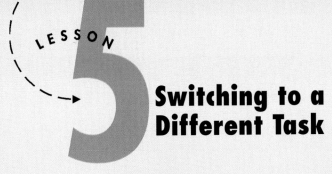

Switching to a Different Task

In Windows 95 lingo, every program you have running represents a different *task*. If you're trying to do several things at once, naturally you'll need to be able to switch from task to task without any trouble. Windows makes this easy.

Just Click the Window You Want

When we left off at the end of Lesson 4, you had just started WordPad, on top of Paint and Notepad. Say you wanted to go back to Notepad to keep working on your first document. One way to do that is to click on the window you want in front:

1 Click anywhere in the Notepad window (such as the title bar).

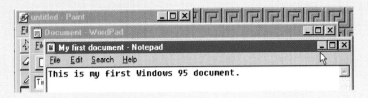

▶ This brings Notepad back to the front.

Or Click the Button on the Taskbar

One of the tricky things about working with a lot of windows at once is that—just as with a messy desk—sometimes an entire window is completely hidden by other windows. (Also, sometimes a window is deliberately hidden; that is to say, *minimized*.)

The purpose of the Taskbar is to make sure that all windows—all tasks—are available at all times.

> **NOTE**
> Notice that the *My first document – Notepad* button on the Taskbar appeared pushed in as soon as you brought Notepad to the front.

1. Click the Minimize button on the Notepad title bar.

▶ Notepad shrinks down to the Taskbar and WordPad is once again on top. Now say you want to return to Notepad. You can't click in its window, can you?

2. Click the *My first document – Notepad* button on the Taskbar.

▶ The Notepad window reappears on top. Try this with the other programs currently running.

3. Click the *Document – WordPad* button on the Taskbar.

4. Then click the *untitled – Paint* button on the Taskbar.

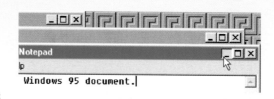

NOTE

Not all dialog boxes show up on the Taskbar, so you may sometimes need to *minimize* some windows, as explained in Lesson 3, in order to get a dialog box to the front.

▶ The untitled – Paint window should now be on top.

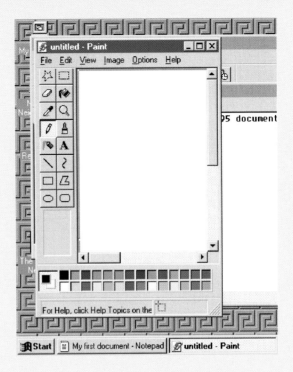

Cycling through All the Tasks

There's also a handy keyboard shortcut for switching from task to task. It's especially useful if you're typing and don't want to take your hands from the keyboard.

1 Hold down the Alt key.

NOTE
There are usually Alt keys on both sides of the space bar—try holding down the left Alt key with your left thumb.

2 Without letting go of the Alt key, press and release the Tab key.

NOTE
If you use your left index finger to press Tab (while still holding down the Alt key with your left thumb), you won't need to move your right hand at all.

31

▶ A plaque appears showing icons for all the running programs, with the current one highlighted by a heavy square and named in the panel below.

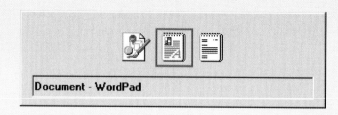

3 Press Tab again to move the highlight to the Notepad icon.

4 Let go of the Alt key and Notepad is once again on top.

Arranging Your Windows

With multiple Windows open, you might concievably want to arrange them evenly or organize them neatly on the desktop. Here's a quick shortcut that can help you do either.

1 First, close the Paint window by clicking the Close button on its title bar.

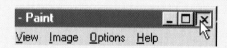

2 Position the mouse pointer over the Taskbar, but not directly over any specific button (there's room to the right of the buttons).

> **NOTE**
>
> The Paint window is not as flexible as most. Because it can't get smaller than a certain minimum size, it's not completely cooperative when it comes to tiling program windows.

3 Click the right mouse button.

▶ A menu pops up.

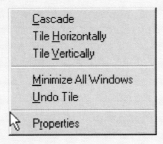

4 Select Tile Horizontally from this menu.

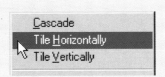

▶ The open windows arrange themselves in a regular *tiled* pattern, covering all the available space on the desktop. (Had you selected Tile Vertically, the results would be similar but the windows would be side by side rather than one on top of the other.)

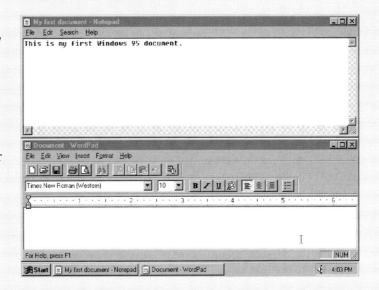

Another approach is to have the windows overlap, but leave the title bar visible for each one. This is called *cascading* the windows, and it's often the best choice for cleaning up a messy desktop when there are many windows open. They can all stay relatively big and you can still click on each window without trouble. Try it with the two windows open now.

5 Right-click the Taskbar again and select Cascade from the menu that pops up.

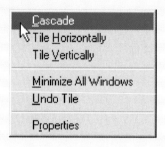

▶ The windows rearrange themselves, this time with one in the upper-left corner and the other in front of it, a little down and to the right.

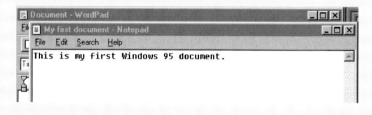

That's all you need to know about juggling several tasks. Now quit both running programs:

6 Click the Close button in the upper-right corner of the Notepad window.

7 Click the Close button in the upper-right corner of the WordPad window.

> **NOTE**
> If you've made any other changes to documents, you'll be asked if you want to save the changes. Unless you've got something important going on, just click No.

5 MINUTES

6 Reopening a Document

If you're like many computer users, you probably don't think in terms of what program you want to run—instead you probably think about the tasks you need to perform, the goals you are trying to accomplish, or the document (or, more likely, *project*) you want to work on.

To accommodate this (more natural, perhaps) way of thinking, Windows 95 enables you to start documents directly, instead of having to poke around for the right program and then open the document. Once again, the Start button is where it all begins.

Clicking Start

We've done this before, so it should be easy.

1 Click the Start button.

2 Move the pointer to the Documents option.

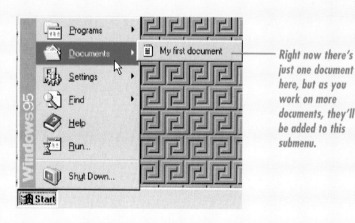

Right now there's just one document here, but as you work on more documents, they'll be added to this submenu.

Clicking the Document

3 Select *My first document*.

▶ The Notepad program starts up with your first document already open.

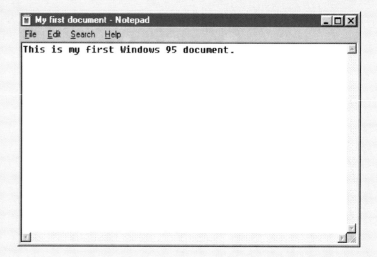

4 Click the Close button to exit the Notepad program again.

With a convenience like that, it's never hard to pick up where you left off.

15 MINUTES

Adding Programs to the Start Menu

The Start button makes it pretty easy to start a program (or a document), but if there's a program you use all the time, you might get tired of going through two or three submenus to get to it.

Fortunately, you're not stuck with the way things are the first time you run Windows. It's very simple to add any program to the Start menu.

Getting to a Program from My Computer

For example, let's say you want to have the Notepad program on your Start menu. First you have to get the program's icon on the screen.

1 Double-click My Computer.

2 In the My Computer window, double-click the (C:) hard drive icon.

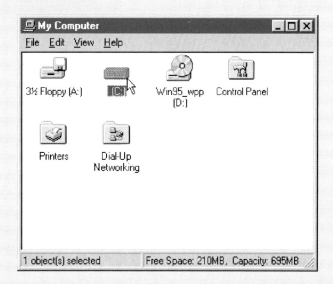

3 In the (C:) window, double-click the Windows folder. As before, your (C:) window will probably have folders and programs in it that are different from mine.

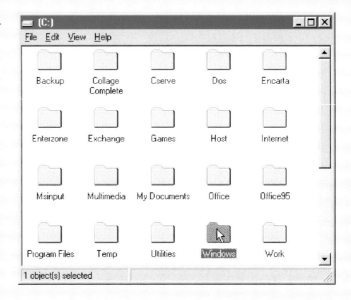

NOTE

If you don't see the Windows folder in the (C:) window, try scrolling to see more folders.

4 In the Windows window, scroll until the Notepad icon appears on the screen (they're in alphabetical order).

The Notepad icon

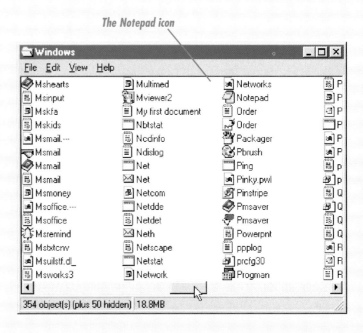

Dragging an Icon onto the Start Button

Now you need to drag the Notepad icon onto the Start button.

1 Click the Notepad icon (and hold down the mouse button).

2 Drag the icon out of the Windows window (keep the mouse button held down). The Notepad icon becomes a *shortcut* as soon as you drag it out of the window (see Lesson 20 for more on shortcuts).

3 Drag it onto the Start button and drop it there (let go of the mouse button).

Now Notepad is right there on the Start menu, ready to run anytime you want.

> **NOTE**
>
> What you just did there is an example of something called *drag and drop*. You can usually move or copy icons or selections from one window to another simply by dragging and dropping. More on this in Lesson 18.

Starting the Program

To see how easy it is to run a program you've put on the Start menu, try it now.

1 Click the Start button, and the Start menu pops up.

2 Click Notepad (at the top of the menu).

▶ Notepad starts up.

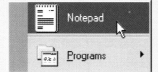

NOTE

Sure, that was easy, but how would you put an icon on the Start menu if you didn't know where it was on the disk? Good question. I'm glad you asked. Lesson 22 explains how to find programs, documents, and other files.

Adding a Program to a Start Menu Submenu

So now you know how to put a program on the Start menu, but what if you don't want to clutter up the main menu and would rather keep useful programs one level down on the Programs submenu? That's almost as easy. Let's put the WordPad program there.

1 Right-click the Start button.

▶ A menu pops up.

2 Click Open from this menu.

▶ A window called Start
Menu appears on the
screen.

*This Notepad icon was put here
when you dragged the shortcut
onto the Start button earlier.*

3 Double-click the Programs
folder. (The folder looks a
little unusual—its icon includes an image of an open
window—to signify that it
is a Start Menu folder.)

▶ The Programs window
opens. Each icon in this
window corresponds to an
option on the Programs
submenu of the Start menu.
The special folder icons
indicate further submenus.

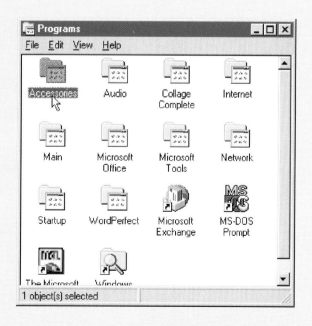

4 Double-click the
Accessories folder.

▶ The Accessories window opens.

5 Scroll down to the bottom of the window, if necessary, to show the WordPad shortcut icon.

The WordPad shortcut icon

6 Right-click the WordPad icon.

▶ A menu pops up.

7 Click Copy from this menu.

8 Press Backspace to return to the Programs window (Backspace always takes you "up" one level in folder windows).

9 Right-click anywhere inside the Programs window.

▶ A menu pops up.

10 Click Paste.

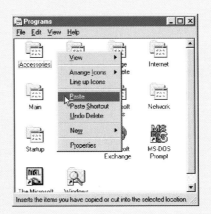

▶ A copy of the WordPad shortcut appears in the Programs window. Don't worry about where it lands.

Now you just have to clean up the Desktop:

11 Click the Accessories window.

12 Hold down the Shift key and click the Close button in the Accessories title bar.

> **NOTE**
>
> The steps are just about the same to put *any* program on any Start menu submenu. See Lessons 16 and 18 for more about the windows on your Desktop and the icons in them.

Verify that the Programs submenu of the Start menu now has a WordPad option:

13 Click Start ➤ Programs.

▶ WordPad appears in alphabetical order (after all the folders).

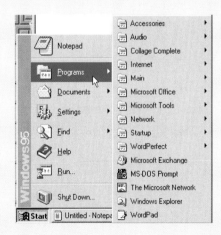

Click anywhere else to close the Start menus.

Removing a Program from a Start Menu Submenu

You remove a program from a Start menu submenu in much the same way: right-click the Start menu to open up the Start Menu window, click the icon for the submenu you want to change (you may have to work your way through several layers), and then drag the shortcut for the program you want to remove to the Recycle Bin (on the Desktop).

When Windows asks you if you're sure you want to do this, click Yes. The shortcut will disappear. After you've closed all the windows, check the Start submenu and you'll see that the program is gone.

> **NOTE**
> Don't worry about the program you "threw away," though. It won't be on that menu anymore, but it's still in your computer. You only threw away a shortcut. Lesson 20 has more on shortcuts and Lesson 23 explains all about throwing away icons, as well as how to "unthrow" them away.

Clearing the Documents Submenu

Here's one other thing you can control on the Start menu. As we discussed in Lesson 6, any document you work with will be added to the Documents submenu of the Start menu. This is an excellent feature, but the menu *can* get cluttered. Fortunately, you can clear that menu out any time you like.

1 Right-click the Taskbar, but not on top of a button.

▶ A menu pops up.

2 Click Properties.

▶ The Taskbar Properties dialog box appears.

3 Click the Start Menu Programs tab.

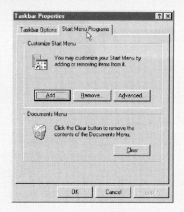

4 Click the Clear button in the Documents Menu area.

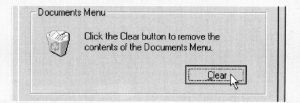

5 Click OK.

6 Click Start ➤ Documents.

▶ The Documents submenu comes up empty.

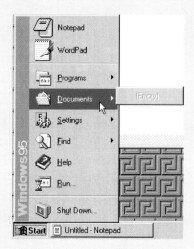

NOTE
We'll be spending some more time at the Taskbar Properties dialog box in the next lesson.

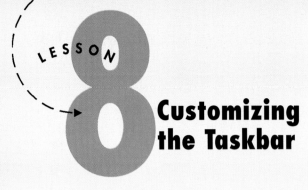

5 MINUTES

LESSON 8

Customizing the Taskbar

By now you may have noticed that the Taskbar is omnipresent. That's one of its main benefits. You can always find it. But if you're not completely happy with the way it looks, where it is, or even with the space it takes up on the screen, you can change any of those things.

Moving the Taskbar

The bottom of the screen is a perfectly decent place to have the Taskbar, but if you want to put it elsewhere, you can. Some might prefer it at the top of the screen, so that the Start menu pulls *down* as most other menus do.

1 Click the Taskbar in a neutral area and hold down the mouse button.

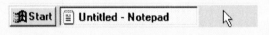

NOTE
Don't click on one of the buttons. The space just to the left of the clock area will do.

2 Drag the pointer toward the top of the screen.

▶ As you begin to move the pointer, a ghost outline of the Taskbar appears. When you get near the top of the screen, the ghost image flicks up there.

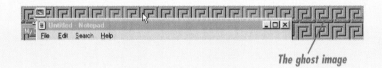

The ghost image

NOTE
If you pass close to one of the sides, the ghost attaches itself there until the pointer gets closer to the top.

▶ The Taskbar moves to the top of the screen and the windows and icons on the screen move down to accommodate it.

3 Click Start ➤ Notepad to see how the Start menu behaves up there.

▶ Another copy of the Notepad program starts. (Of course, your windows will probably appear in different spots on the screen.)

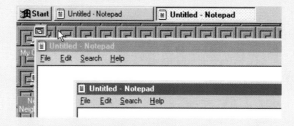

4 Now click the Taskbar (again in a neutral area) and drag it to the left side of the screen. Notice how the windows on the screen slide over to make room for the Taskbar.

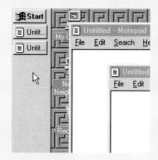

5 Now put the Taskbar back at the bottom of the screen.

Resizing the Taskbar

With more than four or so tasks running, the Taskbar starts to get a bit crowded. It's hard to read the descriptions on most of the buttons. Imagine how hard it would be if you had sixteen windows open!

Fortunately, any time the Taskbar is looking a little scrunched, you can widen it to make room for all the buttons (of course, the trade-off is less room on the screen for other work). Try crowding up the Taskbar now.

1 Double-click the My Computer icon to open its window.

2 Double-click the (C:) hard drive icon to open its window.

3 Double-click the Windows icon to open its window.

▶ Now the Taskbar looks kind of busy.

4 Move the mouse pointer to the top edge of the Taskbar (it will change to a resizing pointer).

5 Drag the pointer up a little ways until the ghost edge of the Taskbar jumps up about half an inch.

6 Release the mouse button, and the Taskbar resizes itself, giving its buttons more breathing room.

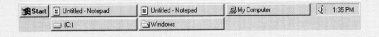

7 Click the edge of the Taskbar and drag it back down to its original size.

NOTE
When the Taskbar is on one of the sides of the screen, you can drag it to any specific width (up to about half the width of the screen—not that you'd want it that wide).

Working around the Taskbar

Even at its basic small size, you still may feel that the Taskbar is in your way. If so, there are a few things you can do to make it less obtrusive. You may or may not have noticed that, in its natural state, the Taskbar always sits in front of everything else on the screen. (There's no reason that you would notice this unless you've moved a window or icon to the bottom edge of the screen.)

1 Click the title bar of one of the Notepad windows and drag the window until its bottom edge slides under the Taskbar.

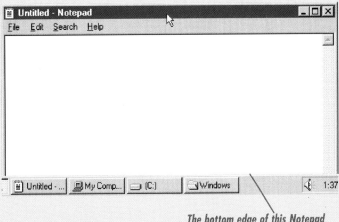

The bottom edge of this Notepad window is now under the Taskbar.

2 Click Start ➤ Settings ➤ Taskbar.

The ellipsis (...) after Taskbar means that this option brings up a dialog box.

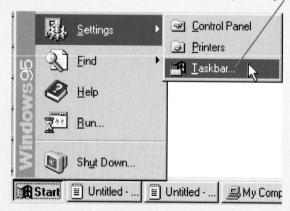

▶ This brings up the Taskbar Properties dialog box.

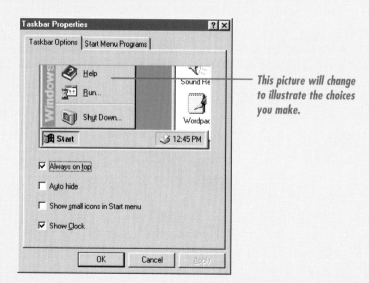

This picture will change to illustrate the choices you make.

NOTE

As you saw in Lesson 7, you can also get to the Taskbar Properties dialog box by right-clicking on the Taskbar and selecting Properties from the menu that pops up.

You have two choices related to keeping the Taskbar out of the way. Of the options in the Taskbar Options tab of the Taskbar Properties dialog box, notice that *Always on top* is already checked.

3 Click *Always on top* (either click the words themselves or click the check box) to uncheck the check box.

4 Click OK (at the bottom of the dialog box).

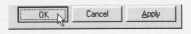

But wait, the Notepad window is still beneath the Taskbar. That's because the Taskbar is the last part of the Desktop you touched.

5 Click the Notepad window and it moves to the front.

> **NOTE**
> The Taskbar will still come to the front if you click it, but it will no longer stay in front automatically.

The other way to keep the Taskbar from getting in the way is to *hide* it.

6 Click Start ➤ Settings ➤ Taskbar.

7 Recheck *Always on top*.

8 Check *Auto hide* (the next option down).

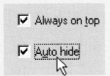

9 Click OK.

51

▶ As soon as you move the pointer away from the Task-bar, the Taskbar disappears.

The Taskbar is now represented by this tiny, almost invisible gray strip at the bottom of the scrreen.

NOTE

The Taskbar will still stay on the screen whenever it is "live" (that is to say, clicked more recently than any other screen object).

So where did it go? It's still there, just out of the way until you need it.

10 Move the mouse pointer to the bottom edge of the screen to make the Taskbar pop up.

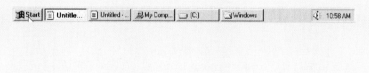

11 Click Start ➤ Settings ➤ Taskbar.

12 Uncheck Auto hide.

13 Click OK.

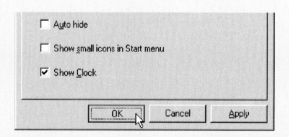

By the way, you can also click the Apply button (in the lower-right corner of the Taskbar Properties dialog box) to fix a setting that you've chosen without closing the window (in case you have other things you want to do in that dialog box).

NOTE
If you find the Start menu to be a little too big and bold, you can effectively shrink it by checking *Show small icons in Start menu* in the Taskbar Properties dialog box (you can see the effects in the preview illustration and then uncheck it again). If you don't want the clock always telling you the time in the lower right, you can uncheck *Show Clock*. But leave those settings as is for now so that your screen will match this book.

Clean up the Desktop now:

14 Click the Windows button on the Taskbar to bring the Windows window to the fore.

15 Shift-click the Close button on the title bar of the Windows window to close it, along with (C:) and My Computer.

16 Close both Notepad windows.

Now you know how to make the Taskbar look, and work, the way you like.

5 MINUTES

Changing the Appearance of Your Desktop

One of the ways to make your computer more comfortable to work with is to customize the appearance of the Windows 95 Desktop and other features. This is now very easy to do.

Changing the Desktop's Background

To change the Desktop's background, follow these steps:

1 Right-click the Desktop.

2 Select Properties from the menu that pops up.

Arrange Icons ▸
Line up Icons

Paste
Paste Shortcut

New ▸

Properties

▶ The Display Properties dialog box appears, with the Background tab selected.

Egyptian Stone is the brown wallpaper pattern you've seen in the shots of my screen. You may have something else selected here, or perhaps (None).

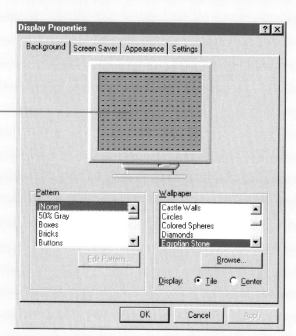

Display Properties

Background | Screen Saver | Appearance | Settings

Pattern
[None]
50% Gray
Boxes
Bricks
Buttons

Edit Pattern...

Wallpaper
Castle Walls
Circles
Colored Spheres
Diamonds
Egyptian Stone

Browse...

Display: ○ Tile ○ Center

OK   Cancel   Apply

> **NOTE**
> Another tab could be selected if you or anyone else has already visited this dialog box. If so, it's no problem. Just click the Background tab to bring it to the front.

3 Scroll through the Wallpaper box and select Squares.

▶ The purple squares pattern appears in the preview (the picture of a computer monitor).

4 Click the Apply button in the lower-right corner of the Display Properties dialog box.

▶ The background appears on your Desktop.

> **NOTE**
> The Apply button applies whatever settings you have chosen without closing the dialog box. (OK would also apply your settings but would close the dialog box.)

Changing the Windows Color Scheme

You can also choose different color schemes from the Display Properties dialog box.

1 Click the Appearance tab.

▶ The Appearance tab comes to the fore, showing various types of windows in the preview area, illustrating the Windows Standard color scheme.

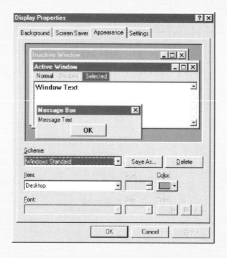

2 Click the little arrow button to the right of the words *Windows Standard* in the Scheme box to drop down the list box.

3 Scroll up through the list box and click Rose (not the *large* version of Rose).

4 Click the Apply button.

▶ The Rose color scheme is applied to Windows, changing even the appearance of the Display Properties dialog box you're currently working in. Not only colors are different in this scheme: the text (in the title bars) is different as well.

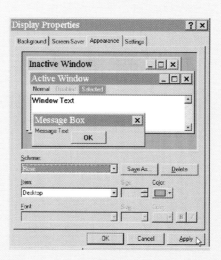

Changing the Sharpness of the Screen Image

Depending on the video capabilities of your computer, you might be able to choose a higher resolution for your screen. *Resolution* means the degree of sharpness, literally the number of dots (*pixels*) that will fit on the screen. The trade-off with higher resolution is that text and images appear smaller.

1 Click the Settings tab.

▶ The Settings tab comes to the fore, showing a generic Windows Desktop in the preview area.

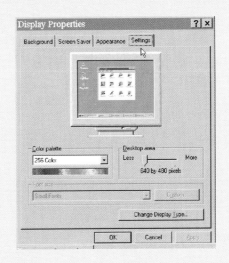

2 Click the slider in the *Desktop area* and drag it from the end marked *Less* (640 by 480 pixels) to the middle (800 by 600 pixels).

3 Click OK.

NOTE

If your slider is unable to move, then your monitor can only display in the resolution you see right now. The good news is that you're done with this lesson (almost)! Jump ahead to "Restoring Your Normal Settings," but skip steps 2 and 3.

▶ Windows brings up a warning dialog box telling you that the screen might flicker when it changes to the higher resolution (it will).

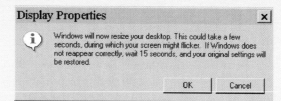

NOTE

If Windows presents you with a dialog box asking you to select your monitor type, then your system is not fully set up for resolution changes, and you should click Cancel. Find the person who installed Windows for you and ask them to install your monitor for Windows 95. (Close the Display Properties dialog box and skip the rest of this lesson.)

4 Click OK.

▶ Your screen will flicker and then the Desktop will reappear at the new resolution (or it will fail to do so if your computer is not equipped for higher resolution).

NOTE

If your Desktop fails to reappear, just wait 15 seconds while it restores itself to its previous state. Then skip to the next section.

5 Windows will ask you if you want to keep this setting. Click Yes.

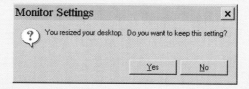

6 Click OK.

▶ The Display Properties dialog box closes and you can now see your modified Desktop.

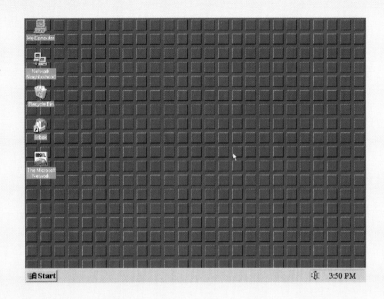

Restoring Your Normal Settings

Putting things back the way they were is just as easy. We'll undo the changes more or less in reverse.

1 Right-click the Desktop and select Properties from the menu that pops up.

2 Click the Settings tab in the Display Properties dialog box.

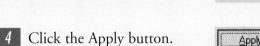

3 Reset the Desktop area slider to 640 by 480 pixels.

4 Click the Apply button.

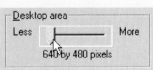

59

5 Click OK when warned about the change.

6 Click Yes after the Desktop flickers and changes.

7 Click the Appearance tab.

8 Click the drop down list box in the Scheme area, scroll through it, and select Windows Standard.

9 Click Apply.

10 Click the Background tab.

11 Scroll to the top of the Wallpaper list box and select (None).

▶ Now my Desktop will look just about the same as yours.

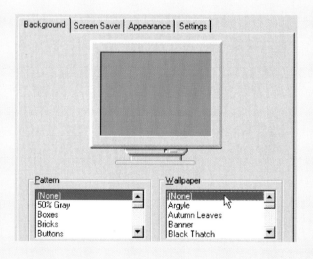

12 Click OK.

▶ Your basic Desktop will be restored.

Feel free to experiment and change your settings as often as you like. The point is to make the computer more pleasant and enjoyable to work with.

10

Getting Help

5 MINUTES

Windows comes with an elaborate online help system. For some people, on-line help is just another annoying extension of those cryptic manuals that come with every piece of hardware and software and are nearly impossible to read. To others, online help is useful because it appears right there on the screen (OK, maybe covering the window you need to look at) and is easier to search through than a heavy manual.

I'm not sure how useful you'll find the Help system, but I owe it to you to point it out and show you how to use it. It's always worth a try when you're stumped.

Help Is on the Start Menu

As with all of these most basic and most useful features of your computer, Help can be found on the Start menu.

1 Click the Start button.

2 Select Help.

▶ If this is the first time you've looked at Windows Help, a Setting Up Help window will appear showing a book being written by a disembodied pen.

Choosing a Topic

▶ A dialog box called Help Topics: Windows Help will next appear, with its Index tab selected. Your other choices at this point are to select the Contents tab and proceed from a top-down outline of the help materials, or to select the Find tab and wait while Help sets up a database of every single word in the help files to enable you to search. The index should be just fine (click it if it's not the one on top).

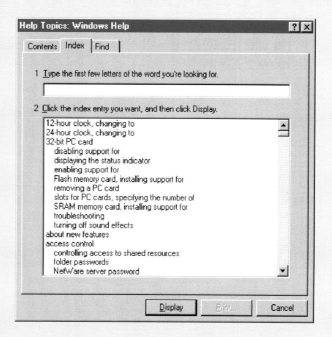

3 Type the word help (it will appear in the box that reads *Type the first few letters of the word you're looking for*).

4 Press Enter.

▶ The Topics Found dialog box will appear, showing topics related to the word you type.

5 Select *Finding similar topics*.

6 Click the Display button.

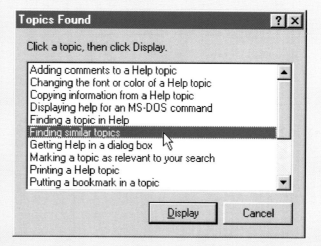

▶ A Windows Help window appears, with step-by-step instructions. Any green underlined words can be clicked to display definitions or take you to different topics.

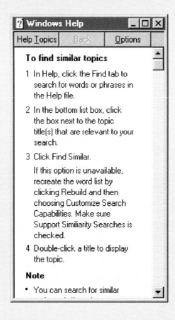

If the topic you get to doesn't answer your question, or if you have other issues you want help with, you can get back to the Help Topics window to try again.

7 Click the Help Topics button at the top of the Windows Help window.

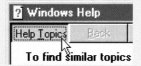

Help with Dialog Boxes

Most Windows dialog boxes now have a What's This? button in the upper-right corner, just to the left of the Close button (it sports a question mark). It enables you to point at areas of the dialog box and get explanations.

1 Click the What's This? button in the upper-right corner of the Help Topics dialog box.

64

2 Move the pointer over to the *Type the first few letters...* box.

▶ The pointer changes to an arrow with a question mark.

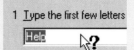

1 Type the first few letters

Help

3 Click in the box.

▶ An explanation pops up. If you click anywhere else the box will disappear.

Displays the Help Index. Type a topic you want to find, or scroll through the list of index entries. Click the index entry you want, and then click Display.

Getting Help Off the Screen

If you've gotten the answers to your questions, you can close the Help windows.

1 Click the Close button in the upper-right corner of the Help Topics dialog box (the Cancel button in the bottom-right would work just as well).

▶ The Help Topics dialog box closes but the Windows Help window lingers on.

2 Click the Close button in the Windows Help window.

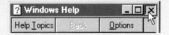

Windows Help

Help Topics   Back   Options

Online help works the same way for all Windows programs (except you generally start it from the Help menu of the program you're running), so you now know how to get help no matter what you're doing in Windows 95.

Shutting Down Your Computer

When the time comes for you to quit working on your computer and walk away from it, you'll probably want to turn it off. But your computer isn't like a stereo, and it's not safe to just flick the on-off switch when you're done with it. Windows needs the opportunity to tidy up a bit and make sure there are no loose ends that might mess you up next time you turn the thing on.

Start Shutting Down

Even though you're now stopping things, you'll still find the command you want on the Start menu.

1 Click the Start button.

2 Select Shut Down (the bottommost option).

▶ Windows will gray out the Desktop and display the Shut Down Windows dialog box. Most of the time, the selected option (*Shut down the computer?*) will suffice. Occasionally, you might want to restart your computer (have it shut down and then automatically start up again), when, for example, you've installed a new program. Ignore the third option (*Restart the computer in MS-DOS mode?*)—only advanced users need it. If you share your computer with other users, each of whom logs in with a different name, then you might sometimes want to choose the last option (*Close all programs and log on as a different user?*), or you may not have this option at all.

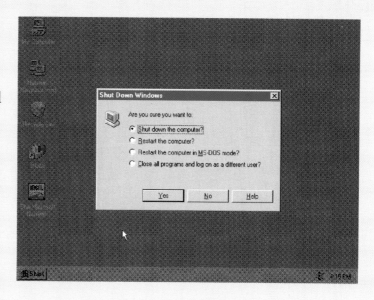

3 Click Yes.

▶ Windows will display a screen letting you know that it's shutting down your computer.

▶ After a while it will tell you
that it's safe to turn your
computer off.

It's now safe to turn off
your computer.

Go ahead and turn it off and then go outside and do something fun that uses your whole body.

PART THREE

Getting Things Done within Programs

To get anything useful done on your computer, you'll have to run a program, such as a word processor, an e-mail program, or a spreadsheet. In Windows, all the most common procedures are virtually the same in just about every program. This part tells you how to save your work, open a saved document, print out your results, and close a document, with or without quitting the program you're running.

Creating a
New Document

So far you've taken a look at Windows itself and all the things you can do with the Start button, you've run some programs, and you've created a document. Now we're going to take a closer look at documents. From the Windows point of view, there are really only a few "things" on your computer. There are folders (also sometimes called *directories*), programs, and documents.

Folders, as we've already seen (and will get a chance to play around with in Part 4), can contain programs, documents, or other folders. That's all they do, really: contain things. Programs are the workhorses of your computer. They do things. You run them and you use them to do work, to create (that's right) documents. So documents are creations. They can also be thought of as saved records of work done. Geeky types think of them as *files* that contain *data*.

Windows 95 represents all of these "things"—folders, programs, and documents—as icons. In addition to running your programs for you (remember the Start button), Windows also lets you act directly on documents themselves.

Turn Everything On

We left off at the end of Lesson 11 with your computer off. Needless to say, you'll need to turn your computer back on and let Windows start up again (see Lesson 1 for a refresher, if you like).

Saving a Document

Making a new document works out to the same thing as saving a new document. Back in Lesson 4 you ran the Notepad program, did some typing, and then saved your work as *My first document*. We went through that sort of quickly at the time, and I promised you'd get a more thorough look at saving a little later. Well, here we are.

Running a Program First

Start Notepad.

1 Click Start ➤ Notepad.

▶ A new (untitled) Notepad window appears.

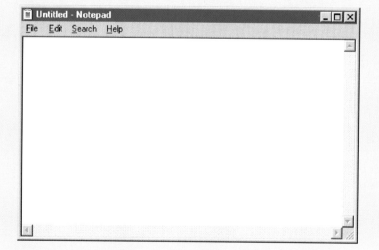

2 Type My second Notepad document is about as interesting as my first one was.

▶ The words will run longer than the width of the window and scroll off the left side of the window. Notepad can *wrap* words, though, to make them fit the width of the Notepad window.

3 Select Edit ➤ Word Wrap.

4 To save your new document, select File ➤ Save.

➤ The Save As dialog box appears. (The first time you save a new document, you have to save it *as* something, meaning you have to assign it a name. Later, you can choose File ➤ Save to save the changes to a document, and you won't be presented with the Save As dialog box. However, if you want to save a copy of your document under a new name, you can choose File ➤ Save As. The Save As dialog box will appear again, and you can type a new name for the new document you'll be creating based on the old one.)

You'll have different folders in your Windows folder.

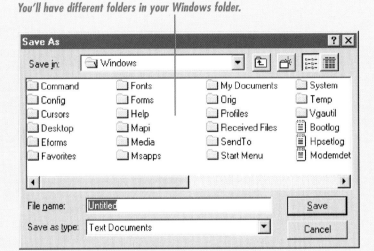

Choosing a Folder

Different programs start you off "aimed at" different folders, meaning that if you choose not to override it, your documents will be saved in some default folder. In the case of Notepad and other Windows accessories, the default is the Windows folder, but that's not usually where you want your documents saved. You'll save the new documents in this lesson onto your Desktop.

1 Click the Up One Level button in the Save As dialog box.

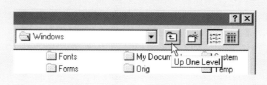

▶ The *Save in* box now shows the hard disk (C:) instead of the Windows folder.

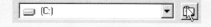

2 Click the button again to go up to the My Computer level.

3 Click the button a final time to get to the Desktop.

4 Type **My Second** (it will show up in the *File name* box).

5 Click the Save button.

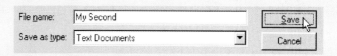

▶ A Notepad icon called My Second appears on your Desktop and the file name My Second replaces the dummy name Untitled on the button in the Taskbar (and in the Notepad title bar).

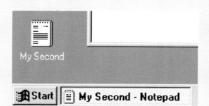

Saving a Document "As" a New Name

Now let's make another copy of this document.

1 Select File ➤ Save As.

▶ The Save As dialog box appears, still "aimed at" the Desktop, now with the My Second document icon appearing in the main window.

2 Type **Another Second**.

3 Click Save.

▶ A Notepad document icon labeled Another Second appears on your Desktop.

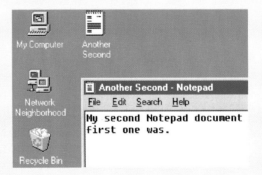

4 Close the Notepad program.

Creating a New Document
on the Desktop

As alluded to at the beginning of this lesson, you can also create a document without first having to run the program it will be associated with. Try this now.

1 Right-click anywhere on the Desktop.

▶ A menu pops up.

2 Select New.

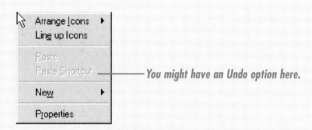

You might have an Undo option here.

▶ A submenu pops up. Your submenu will probably contain a different list of document types (below the line) from mine. It all depends on what programs are installed on your computer and which ones know how to "register" their document types with Windows 95.

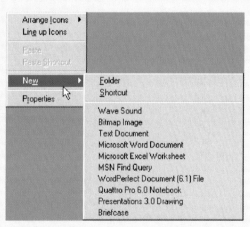

3 Select Bitmap Image. (A bitmap image is the type of document created by the Paint program.)

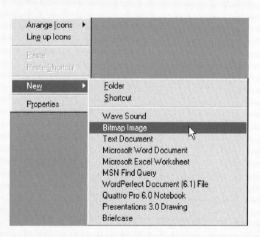

▶ A Paint icon appears on your Desktop wherever your pointer was aimed when you right-clicked it, with the dummy label New Bitmap Image, highlighted.

4 Type **One Hand Clapping**, to give the (so far empty) Paint document a name.

5 Press Enter.

▶ There, now you've created a new document directly on the Desktop, without running any program.

Of course, there's nothing in that document yet. To put something besides a blank bitmap in the document, you first have to open it. Lesson 13 will show you how to open documents.

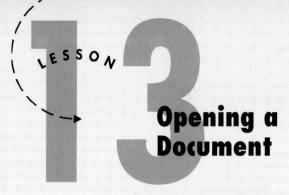

Opening a Document

5 MINUTES

Whether you create a document inside a program (by saving it) or directly on the Desktop (or in a folder window), you have to have the document open before you can add to it or change it. We left off at the end of Lesson 12 with three new icons on the Desktop—two Notepad documents and a Paint document:

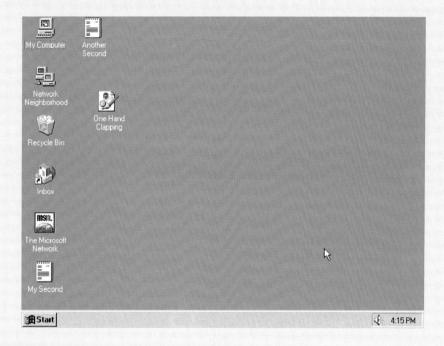

There are several different ways to open documents. You can double-click a document icon. You can right-click a document icon and choose Open. You can run a program and use its File ➤ Open command. If it's one of the last fifteen documents you worked on, you can also select Start ➤ Documents and then choose it from that submenu, as you saw in Lesson 6.

77

> **NOTE**
> The Documents submenu will only list documents from programs that "know how" to have their recent documents listed there. Eventually, all Windows programs will be able to do this, but at first, some of your programs may not.

Let's try a few of these methods.

Opening a Document Directly

Since many of Windows 95's innovations are geared toward allowing you to focus on documents and not hunt around for programs, let's start with opening documents directly.

Double-Clicking an Icon

Let's start with the Paint document, One Hand Clapping. Remember, you created that without ever running the Paint program.

1 Double-click the One Hand Clapping icon on your Desktop.

▶ The Paint program starts up with the (blank) One Hand Clapping document open. (You've got to have the program running to actually view, print, or change a document.)

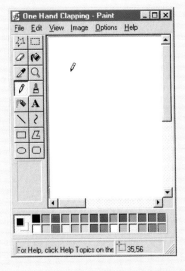

2 Draw your impression of one hand clapping. Don't worry, you won't be graded on your artwork—in fact, I'll do my drawing with my right hand (I'm left-handed), and I'll only use the pencil tool.

3 Now we want to hide the Paint window to keep the Desktop icons available. Click the Minimize button in the Paint title bar.

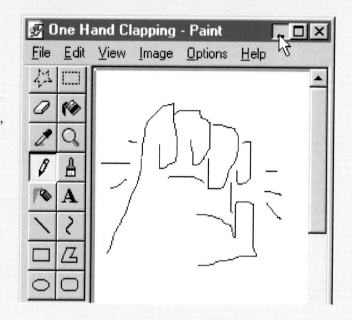

Right-Clicking an Icon

Now let's try it with right-clicking. There's no special advantage to doing it this way, but it's a good habit to try right-clicking every element on the Windows screen. Usually, just about anything you'd want to do with the icon you're clicking will appear on the menu that pops up.

1 Right-click the Another Second document icon.

▶ A menu pops up.

2 Select Open.

▶ A Notepad window appears with the Another Second document open.

Running a Program First

As mentioned before, you can also run a program and then open a document from within the program you're running. This is the more traditional approach, and it's most suitable when you already have a program running, or when it's easier to get to and run the program (say, from the Start menu) than it is to find the document icon (if, for example, it's buried under multiple layers of folders).

Running the Same Program the Document Was Made In

Normally, you'll want to open a document in the program it was made in. In fact, some documents simply can't be opened by other programs. Let's open another one of those Notepad documents we created, starting from scratch. (We could open a document in the Notepad window that's already open, but Notepad can only keep one document open at a time, so that would have the effect of closing the first document.)

1 Select Start ➤ Notepad. (Remember, you put Notepad on the Start menu in Lesson 7.)

▶ A new blank Notepad window appears.

2 Select File ➤ Open.

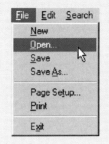

▶ The Open dialog box appears. It bears a striking resemblance to the Save As dialog box and it's also "aimed at" the Windows folder, the way the Save As dialog box was.

3 Click the Up One Level button three times, to (C:), then My Computer, then Desktop.

A Short Digression on Right-Clicking Anywhere

When I said you should experiment with right-clicking all over the Windows 95 screen, I meant it. Just about anywhere you see icons is *hot*, meaning you can right-click the icons to act on them and even right-click the box or area they appear in. Try this now.

1 Right-click in the main area of the Open dialog box.

The window in a dialog box is "hot."

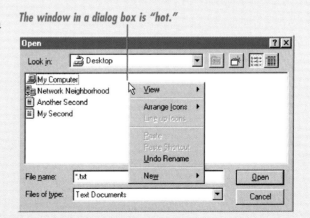

▶ A menu pops up, just as it would on the Desktop (or in a folder window).

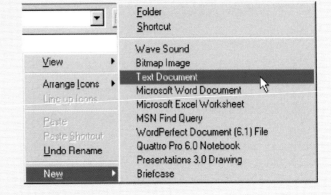

2 Select New.

3 Select Text Document.

▶ A new document icon appears in the box, with a dummy label, New Text Document, highlighted.

4 Type a name for the document, **Another blank one**, and press Enter.

Now Back to Your Regularly Scheduled Document-Opening

Heck, why not open the new blank document you just created?

1 If *Another blank one* is not still highlighted, select it.

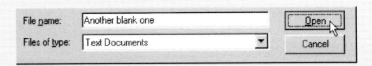

2 Click the Open button.

Notepad opens the blank document. (Nothing appears in the Notepad window, of course, since that document is blank, but its name appears in the title bar.) Now close the document. Go ahead and close the other Notepad document (the one containing Another Second) too.

Opening a Document in a Different Program

If you want to open a document in a different program, you must run that other program first, since double-clicking (or right-clicking and choosing Open) on the document will automatically start the program it was created in (or created for). When would you want to do this? Well, sometimes you'll want to open a text file in a more sophisticated word processor. Notepad can't even do simple things like search for text and replace it with other text.

Try opening a Notepad document in WordPad.

1 Click Start ➤ Programs ➤ WordPad. (Remember, you put WordPad on the Programs submenu in Lesson 7.)

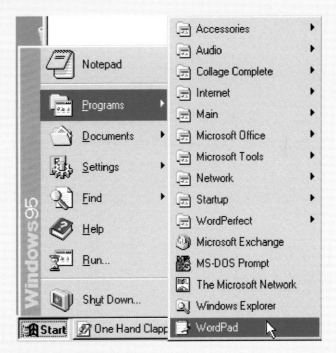

▶ A blank WordPad window appears on the screen. Instead of *Untitled*, WordPad uses the more elegant *Document* as its dummy name when no document is open.

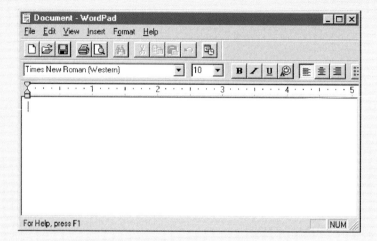

2 Click the Open button in the WordPad toolbar (it's just under the Edit menu name).

NOTE

Many programs have a shortcut button such as this one for opening documents. The image on it is usually some variation on the theme of a folder being opened.

▶ The Open dialog box appears, looking very similar to its counterpart from the Notepad program. WordPad, another accessory, also starts you off aimed at the Windows folder.

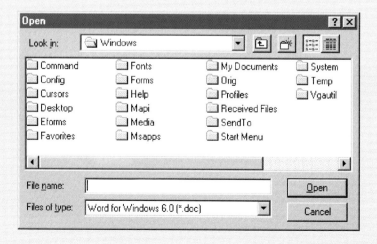

3 Click the Up One Level button three times to get to the Desktop.

▶ No documents appear because the Open dialog box is looking for Word for Windows documents (look in the *Files of type* box at the bottom of the dialog box).

4 Click the Files of type box to drop down a list, and choose Text Documents.

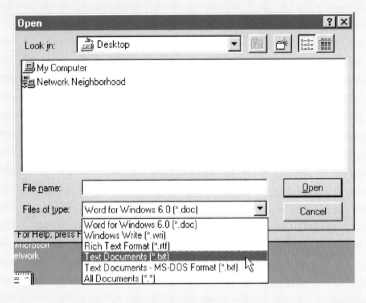

▶ Now the text documents appear in the window.

5 Select the My Second document icon.

6 Click Open.

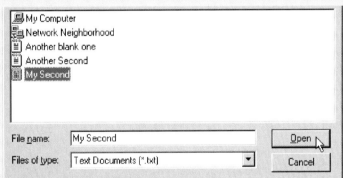

▶ The text document opens in the WordPad window. OK, so it's not so exciting. At least now you know it can be done. Show's over.

So now you've made some documents, and you've opened them up. What about getting the information in them out of the computer and into the real world? You can do that by printing or faxing, both of which are covered in Lesson 14.

14 Printing or Faxing a Document

5 MINUTES

Most people use their computers as typewriters (for the most part), writing documents and then printing them out. Without a printer, therefore, a computer is nearly useless, at least for most of us. So you need to know how to print your documents. As usual, you can do this from within a program, or by acting directly on an icon.

Printing from within a Program

If you happen to have the program already running with your document open in it, there's no reason not to print directly from within the program. Try it now with the My Second document in the WordPad program.

1 Click the *My Second – WordPad* button on the Taskbar to make sure the WordPad document is in front.

2 Click the Printer button on the WordPad toolbar (it looks like a little laser printer). Many programs provide similar shortcuts for printing. If you see no button like this when you're trying to print from within a program, pull down the File menu and select Print. Usually you'll then have to click another button on a Print dialog box, one that

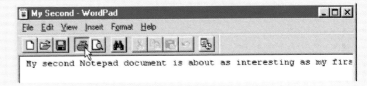

says Print or OK or Go for
it, or something like that.

> **NOTE**
>
> You'll notice that the sentence that we wrapped earlier is no longer wrapped—it goes off
> the page. Unfortunately, the word wrap feature doesn't last from one Notepad session
> to the next.

The document prints and you waste a sheet of paper. Now close the WordPad window
(and thereby exit WordPad).

3 Click the Close button in
the WordPad title bar.

Printing Directly from an Icon

As I keep harping on, Windows now lets you perform most actions directly on document icons, allowing you to forget about the programs used to create the documents, except when absolutely necessary (such as when you are working on the contents of the document). Therefore, you can print a document without first running the program it was created in. Try this now with the My Second document on the Desktop.

1 Right-click the My Second
document icon.

▶ A menu pops up.

2 Select Print.

> **NOTE**
>
> If you watch carefully immediately after selecting Print, you'll see that Windows does actually start up the Notepad program in order to print the document. Still, you didn't have to do it.

The document prints again and you waste yet another sheet of paper. The document looks a little different the second time you print it, because Notepad automatically puts the title of the document at the top of the page (and the word Page and a page number centered at the bottom).

> **NOTE**
> If you put a shortcut icon for your printer on the Desktop, you can drag a document onto it and it will print automatically. See Lesson 20 for more on creating shortcuts.

Faxing a Document

If you've got a fax/modem built into your computer (or attached to it), then you can fax your documents just as easily as printing them. (If you don't have a fax, you might as well skip the rest of this lesson and go on to Lesson 15.)

Try faxing your bitmap Paint picture to an unsuspecting friend.

1 Right-click the One Hand Clapping document icon on the Desktop.

▶ A menu pops up.

2 Select Send To ➤ Fax Recipient.

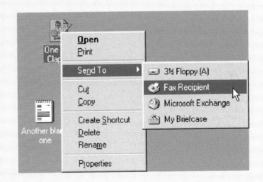

> **NOTE**
> Just as with printers, if you put a shortcut icon for your fax on the Desktop, you can drag a document onto it and it will start the fax process automatically. See Lesson 20 for more on creating shortcuts.

▶ This starts up the Compose New Fax wizard, a step-by-step automated process that Windows walks you through. It first asks you where you are (in case you're traveling with a laptop and the number you're faxing might require different handling of the area code). If you're sitting at a computer that isn't mobile, you can check the *I'm not using a portable computer, so don't show this to me again* option.

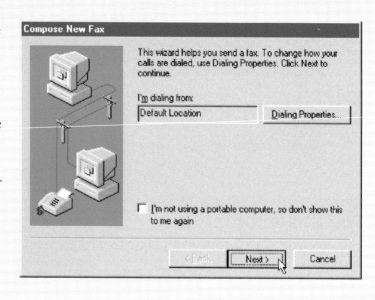

3 Click the Next button.

▶ The dialog box changes. If you've faxed people before and are maintaining an Address Book, you can click the Address Book button and choose your recipient from there.

Please don't send your fax to my friend Dr. Eigenvalue.

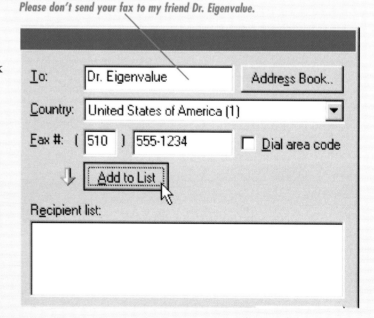

4 Type the name of the recipient in the To box.

5 Click in the Fax # box and type the area code and phone number.

6 Click Add to List.

7 Click Next.

▶ The dialog box changes again. You can choose no cover page for your fax or a different one from the list of options. (Your options may differ from the ones shown here.)

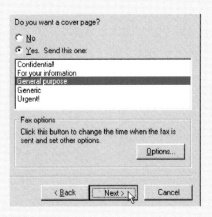

8 Click Next.

▶ The dialog box changes yet again.

9 Type a subject for your fax.

10 Type a short note, if you wish.

11 Click Next.

▶ The dialog box changes one last time. (By the way, at any time you can click the Back button to return to an earlier step in the process and change one of your previous decisions.)

12 Click the Finish button.

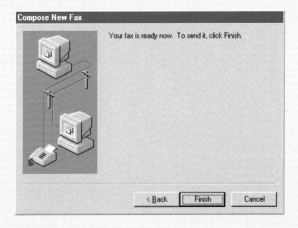

Your document is sent as a fax to the number you entered.

> **NOTE**
> If your fax isn't working right, find the person who installed Windows on your computer and make them figure out what's wrong.

OK, let's see... you've created new documents, opened them, and printed and faxed their contents. What's left? Putting things away when you're done with them, better known as *closing documents*, covered in Lesson 15.

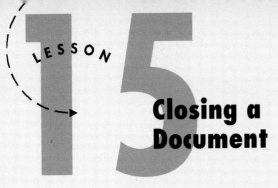

Closing a Document

5 MINUTES

When you're finished with an open document, you need to close it. For some types of documents, this is simply a matter of closing the window of the program showing the open document. This also exits the program. Other programs can have more than one document open at a time and allow you to close a single document without exiting the program. You've closed many program windows already, so I'll show you the variations.

Closing a Minimized Document

If a document (or, technically, the program it's open in) is minimized to the Taskbar, you can close it without first opening it, though admittedly, the difference isn't much.

1 Right-click on the One Hand Clapping button in the Taskbar.

▶ A menu pops up.

2 Select Close.

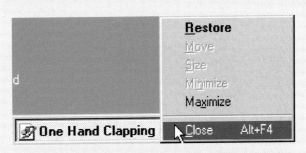

▶ You never saved your changes to the picture, so Paint gives you one last chance to save before quitting.

3 Click Yes.

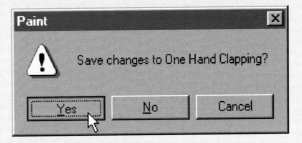

What you just did is exactly equivalent to clicking the Close button in the Paint window title bar. (You can also press Alt+F4, as the pop-up menu shows.)

Closing One of Several Documents without Quitting the Program

Unfortunately, none of the accessories that come with Windows is capable of opening more than a single document at a time. For this next demonstration, I'll have to rely on you either to follow along with Microsoft Word (if you have that program), or to start another word processor (such as WordPerfect). If you haven't got a word processor (for heaven's sake, get one), just skim this section without trying to duplicate the steps.

1 Start your word processor (for me, that means Start ➤ Programs ➤ Microsoft Word).

Your word processor might appear on another menu.

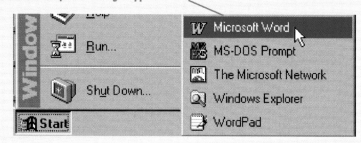

2 Click the Open button in the toolbar.

3 Go "up one level" a few times until you're aimed at the Desktop.

NOTE

By now you should be getting the hang of changing the folder whose contents are shown by the Open dialog box and opening documents. This is one of the things you do over and over so many times that it quickly becomes second nature.

4 Open My Second.

5 Click Open again and open Another Second as well.

6 Now, click the lower of the two Close buttons (the one that appears on the menu bar and not in the title bar).

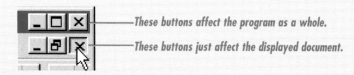

These buttons affect the program as a whole.

These buttons just affect the displayed document.

▶ Another Second closes, leaving the program still running with My Second in the window.

7 Click the main Close button (the one on the title bar).

▶ The program closes, taking My Second with it.

There, now you know just about everything you need to know about documents and their icons. In the next part, you'll be playing around more with the Desktop, with the folders on your computer, and with all the other things you can do with icons.

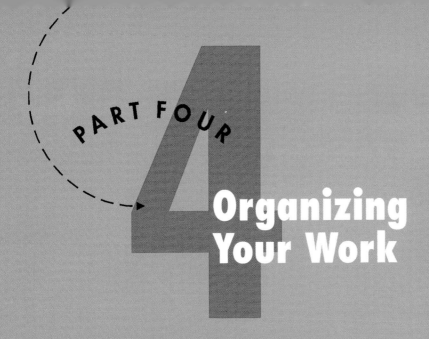

PART FOUR

Organizing Your Work

Like real-world desktops and file folders, computers can often get cluttered and disorganized very quickly. Windows 95 makes it easy to organize your work into folders, and takes all the trouble out of moving, copying, and creating shortcuts to your important work. This part shows you how to work with icons (the symbolic representations of programs), documents, folders, and shortcuts; how to find missing files; and how to throw away (and retrieve) files.

What's On My Computer?

10 MINUTES

By now you've learned to rely on the Start menu for running programs, opening documents, shutting down your computer, and so on. You've also now had a chance to see all the things you can do directly to documents. In the course of all this experimentation, you've been dealing with the Desktop and the My Computer icon a little, but without much explanation.

The live Desktop is perhaps the most significant new feature of Windows 95. The most important icon on the Desktop is the My Computer icon. To take full advantage of Windows, you'll need to be comfortable with opening My Computer, changing the appearance of icons and windows, and rooting around through levels of folders for programs or documents.

My Computer and Desktop Windows

My Computer, as you recall, opens up into a window, as do all of the other icons inside it. These windows all behave similarly, in predictable ways.

Opening My Computer

Start by opening My Computer and taking another look at the windows that appear on your Desktop.

1 Double-click the My Computer icon.

My Computer

▶ The My Computer window opens on your Desktop, still in the size and shape you left it last. Didn't it look better when its size was more compact and the icons in it lined up in two rows? (Remember, you may not have the same set of icons that I have on my computer. You probably have floppy drive and hard drive icons, and the Control Panel and Printers system folders, but you may not have a CD-ROM drive or a Dial-Up Networking system folder.)

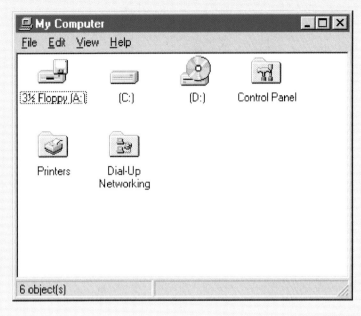

2 Click the bottom-right corner of the window and drag it back to its original size.

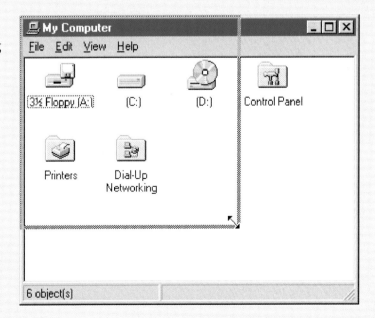

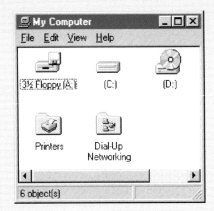

▶ Your icons may not realign themselves to fit the new window shape. This depends on how the View options are set in this window. On my screen, the Control Panel system folder does not show up in the window (but the scroll bar at the bottom of the window gives away its location—it's just off the right side of the window).

Arranging Icons in a Window

One way to get icons to fit in a window best as they can is to turn on the Auto Arrange feature.

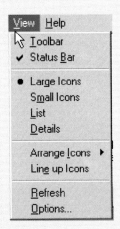

1 Click the View menu in the My Computer window's menu bar.

▶ A menu drops down, showing commands that control the appearance of the window (Toolbar, Status Bar), commands that control the appearance of the icons in the window (Large Icons, Small Icons, List, Details), commands that control the arrangement of the icons

(Arrange Icons, Line up Icons), and two miscellaneous commands (Refresh, Options). Only one of the icon appearance commands can be selected at once, hence the large bullet to the left of the Large Icons option.

> **NOTE**
> You choose the Refresh command when you've performed some other action that has changed the contents of a window, to make the window update itself and reflect the change.

2 Select Arrange Icons.

▶ A submenu pops up.

3 Select Auto Arrange (unless it's already checked—then, just click outside the menu and choose nothing).

The icons will fit themselves into the window. If the scroll bar(s) still appears at the edge(s) of the window, drag the window's bottom-right corner down and away a little to allow enough room for the icons.

Opening the Hard Drive (C:)

The My Computer window purports to show you the contents of your computer, but for most purposes it's your hard drive (C:) that contains what you're looking for. As usual, there are several ways to open the hard drive window. You've already double-clicked the icon in earlier lessons to open it. Naturally, right-clicking will also work.

1 Right-click the (C:) icon.

▶ A menu pops up, featuring most of the things anyone would want to do with a hard-drive icon.

2 Click elsewhere to close the menu.

3 Now click the File menu.

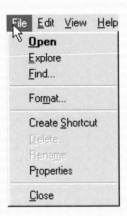

▶ A menu drops down featuring all of the options from the pop-up menu as well as a few additional options (some grayed out, meaning currently unavailable).

4 Select Open to open the (C:) window.

Removing the Status Bar

The (C:) window has all the same menu options as the My Computer window. Remember those first two options on the View menu that control the appearance of the window? The first puts a toolbar on the window. This toolbar merely duplicates all of the commands in the various menus on the menu bar, so we'll skip it. The Status Bar option is on by default. (The Status Bar is at the bottom of the window, and shows how many objects are in the window and how much disk space is taken up by them.) Try removing it now.

5 Select View ➤ Status Bar.

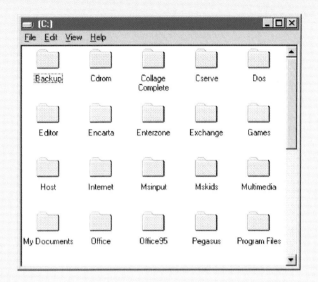

▶ The Status Bar disappears. (As usual, the icons in your hard-drive window will not match mine, though there will be some in common.) If necessary, drag your window so that its size and shape are close to mine, about five icons wide and four high.

Changing the Appearance of Icons

By default, icons in a window will appear as large icons, unless there are so many that Windows makes an assumption and displays them as small icons (so they can fit and be seen more easily). You may recall that the icons in the Windows folder were small the first time you opened that window.

Choosing Small Icons

You can override the default choice at any time.

1 Click View.

2 Select Small Icons.

▶ The icons change to small icons (still depicting the same images, such as folders, logos, and so on), with the file names to their right, rather than below each icon. (The List option in the View menu produces a very similar result, except that the icons are ordered from top to bottom, filling the left column of the window first and then filling each successive column, as needed.)

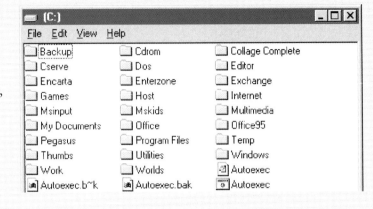

Choosing Details View

The last view option is Details, which devotes a separate line to each icon, with full information about the file the icon represents.

3 Select View ➤ Details.

▶ Each icon now appears with detailed information, but it doesn't all fit in this window size.

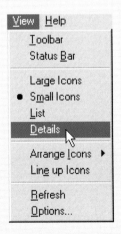

4 Click the Maximize button in the (C:) window's title bar.

5 Drag the scroll box to the bottom of the scroll bar.

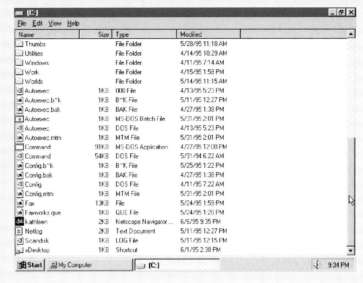

▶ The C: window takes over the whole screen (except for the Taskbar, of course), and you can now clearly see the Name, Size, Type, and Modified information. Modified is short for "the date when the file was last modified." You can click on the dividers between any of those headings and drag them to resize the column to the left.

6 Click the Size header.

▶ The files are organized into size order, from smallest to largest.

7 Click Size again.

▶ The files are now sorted in descending size order.

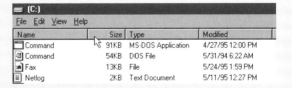

8 Click the Restore button in the (C:) title bar to put the window back to its old size.

Choosing Other View Options

You can also control how the Desktop windows function, what information appears in their title bars, what icons are hidden (if any), and whether or not the old DOS extensions (three-letter abbreviations at the end of each file name) are shown.

First, open another window.

1 Double-click the Windows folder in the (C:) window (scroll up to it first if you need to).

▶ The Windows window opens, with its Status Bar present (choices made for one window don't automatically carry over to others) and its icons small.

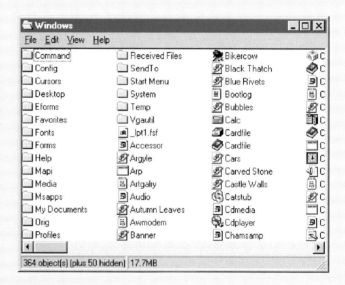

2 Select View ➤ Options.

▶ This brings up the Options dialog box, with its Folder tab in front. There are only two options on this tab, mutually exclusive. The first, *Browse Folders using a separate window for each folder,* is the default. This is the way your folder windows have been working. When you double-clicked Windows, for instance, it opened in its own window. The second option, *Browse folders by using a single window that changes as you open each folder,* has the main advantage of reducing the proliferation of windows on your Desktop, as every new folder opened replaces the old one, opening in the same space. I don't recommend this option.

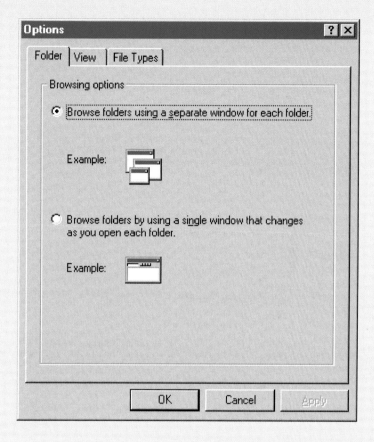

NOTE

Selecting View ➤ Toolbar in any folder window has the same effect as choosing the second option in this dialog box.

3 Click the View tab.

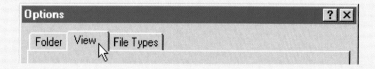

4 Click the *Show all files* radio
button in the Hidden Files
area. (Normally, you don't
want to see the hidden files,
since they're mainly very
technical. I'm just showing
you the alternative. When
would you need to do this?
When you're looking for a
specific, hidden file and
need to see them all.)

5 Uncheck *Hide MS-DOS file
extensions for file types that
are registered.*

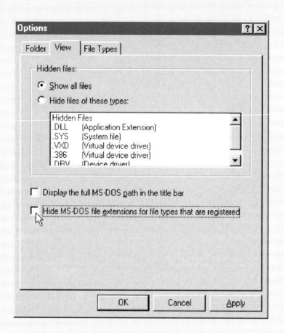

6 Click OK.

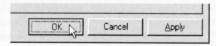

7 Select View ➤ Large Icons.

8 Now scroll through the
Windows window.

▶ Notice how most file names
have some kind of exten-
sion or other after them.
Files with extensions such
as .dll would normally be
hidden.

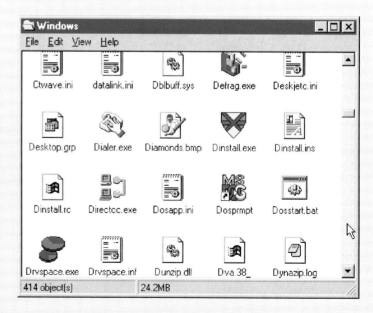

9 Select View ➤ Small Icons.

10 Select View ➤ Options.

11 Click the View tab.

12 Click *Hide files of these types:*.

13 Recheck *Hide MS-DOS etc.*

14 Click OK.

▶ The Windows window appears in its familiar configuration.

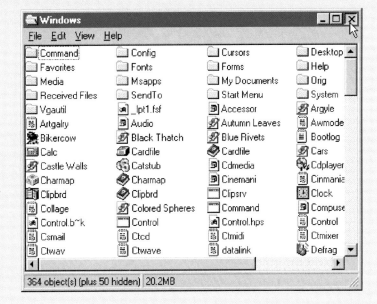

In the next lesson I'll show you how to create folders in windows and on the Desktop and how to move icons around from folder to folder and onto the Desktop.

Making a New Folder

5 MINUTES

The purpose of folders is to provide some organizing structure for your programs and documents. Naturally, your organizational needs will evolve as you work with your computer and, from time to time, you'll need to create new folders to file things away. Making a new folder, either in a window or on the Desktop, is as easy as making a new document.

First, press Backspace to return to the (C:) window.

Making Folders inside of Folders

As with most other Desktop operations, you can make a new folder in a window by choosing an option from the menu bar of the window, or by right-clicking inside the window. Try the first approach now.

1 Select File ➤ New ➤ Folder.

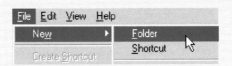

▶ A new folder appears in the window with a dummy name, New Folder, highlighted and ready for renaming.

2 Type **Test** and press Enter.

3 Next, double-click the new Test folder icon.

▶ The empty Test folder window appears.

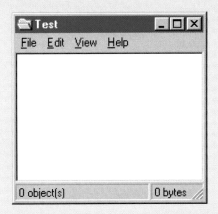

4 Resize and move the (C:) window more or less alongside the Test window.

5 Now right-click inside the Test window.

▶ A menu pops up.

6 Select New ➤ Folder.

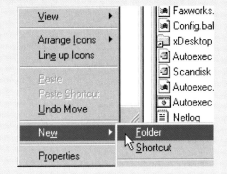

7 Type the name Top Secret for the new folder and press Enter.

111

Making a Folder on the Desktop

You can also make a folder directly on the desktop.

1   Right-click in the area of the Desktop below the Test window.

2   Select New.

3   Select Folder.

4   Type the name Things to do and press Enter.

That wasn't so tough, was it?

Copying and Moving Icons

10 MINUTES

The Desktop and the folder windows that live on it give you total control over the icons they display. That means you can make copies of these icons and put them in other folders (or on the Desktop), and that you can move the icons around between folders (and onto the Desktop).

First, a little maneuvering to set the stage:

1 Open the Windows window (if it's not still open).

2 Shift-click the Close button in the (C:) window to close it and the My Computer window.

3 Now resize and move the Windows window so it sits more or less to the right of the Test window.

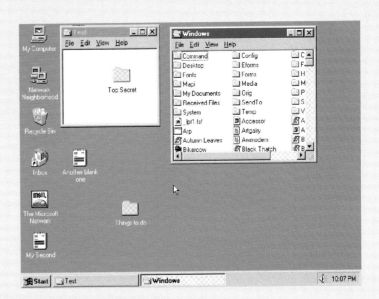

Copying an Icon

Now you can work with one of the Paint documents in the Windows window that's there for use as a backdrop.

Using Copy and Paste

One easy way to copy icons is with the Copy and Paste commands.

1 Click the Autumn Leaves icon.

> **NOTE**
>
> If there's no document in your Windows directory called Autumn Leaves, no matter. You can create one yourself, in name at least. As described in Lesson 21, right-click in the window and select New ➤ Bitmap Image from the menus that pop up. Type Autumn Leaves and press Enter. Voila, a perfectly suitable fake.

2 Pull down the Edit menu and select Copy (notice the Ctrl+C keyboard shortcut suggested on the menu).

3 Click in the Test window.

4 Select Edit ➤ Paste (notice the Ctrl+V keyboard short-cut suggested on the menu) to paste a copy of the document into the Test folder.

5 Now right-click on the Desktop, a little to the right of the *Things to do* folder.

6 Select Paste.

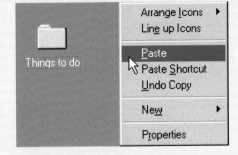

▶ Another copy of the Autumn Leaves document appears on the Desktop where you clicked.

Using Drag and Drop

You can also copy icons using drag and drop, as long as you remember to hold down the Ctrl key the whole time.

1 Double-click the Things to do folder to open the Things to do window.

2 Move the empty Things to do window to a position more or less below the Test window.

3 Hold down the Ctrl key and click the Autumn Leaves icon in the Test window.

115

4 Drag it down to the Things to do window (notice the plus sign that indicates you are dragging a copy and not the original—if you don't see it, start over).

Right-Clicking

As usual, you can achieve the same results by right-clicking the icon you want to copy.

1 Right-click the Autumn Leaves icon in the Things to do window.

2 Select Copy from the menu that pops up.

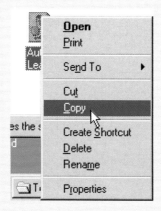

3 Right-click in the Test window and select Paste.

116

▶ A warning dialog box appears because you are trying to copy a file to a place where a file by the same name already exists.

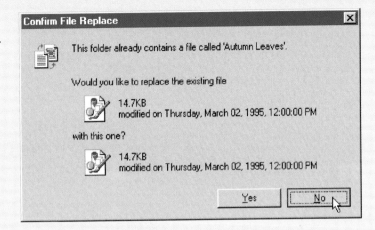

4 Click No.

Moving an Icon

Moving an icon is just as easy, if not easier, than copying one. You can do so with simple drag and drop, with cut and paste, or by right-clicking. Let's start with drag and drop this time.

Using Drag and Drop

Drag the Autumn Leaves icon from the Things to do window to the Test window:

1 Click the Autumn Leaves icon in the Things to do window.

2 Drag it up into the Test window and release the mouse button.

3 This time, click Yes in the
Confirm File Replace dialog
box.

Right-Clicking

By now, you'll have noticed that the right-clicking options always duplicate some of the
menu options, so I won't make you try out *every* alternative.

1 Right-click the Autumn
Leaves icon in the Test
window.

2 Select Cut from the menu
that pops up.

▶ The Autumn Leaves icon
becomes grayed out, to
show that it's been cut (but
not yet pasted).

3 Right-click in the Things to
do window and select Paste.

Copying within a Folder

Here's a handy shortcut for creating a copy of an icon within the same folder.

1 Hold down Ctrl, and click the Autumn Leaves icon in the Things to do window, then drag it slightly to the left.

▶ The copy drag and drop pointer (with plus sign) appears with a ghost copy of the icon.

2 Release the mouse button.

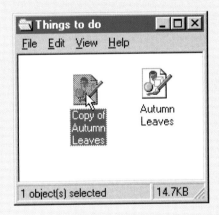

▶ A copy of the icon appears, with the name *Copy of Autumn Leaves* (to avoid a conflict with the original document).

3 Change the document's name to Fall Leaves.

> **NOTE**
>
> You can also use this method (Ctrl-clicking and dragging) to create a copy of an icon in a different folder or on the Desktop.

119

Sneaky Right-Clicking Shortcuts

There's more to right-clicking than letting a menu pop up, though you'd never know it without experimenting. You can also right-click on an icon and then *without releasing the mouse button*, start dragging it.

1 Right-click the Fall Leaves icon.

2 Without releasing the mouse button, drag it onto the Desktop, to the right of the Autumn Leaves document on the Desktop.

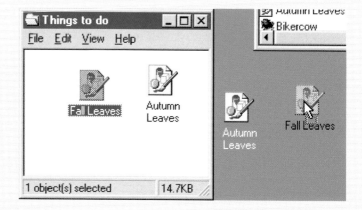

3 Release the mouse button.

▶ A menu pops up, offering you the choice of moving the icon, copying it, making a shortcut, or canceling the operation.

4 Select Copy Here.

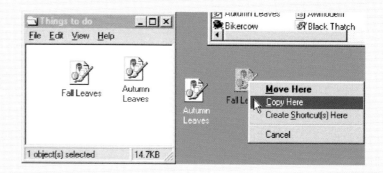

▶ A copy of the document appears on the Desktop.

NOTE
We'll get into shortcuts shortly (in Lesson 20).

Dropping an Icon onto a Folder

You don't have to have a folder window open to drag an icon into it. As long as you have the folder icon itself on the screen, you can simply drag the icon you want to move (or copy) onto the folder.

1 Double-click the Top Secret folder.

▶ The Top Secret window opens (move it to the position shown if it doesn't appear right there).

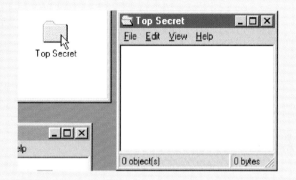

2 Click the Fall Leaves icon on the Desktop and drag it onto the Top Secret folder icon in the Test window.

▶ The Fall Leaves document appears in the Top Secret window.

So there's a full repertoire of copying and moving routines. Normally, I'd prefer to tell you the *best* way (meaning the quickest and easiest), but part of the gestalt of Windows 95 is that the most comfortable or convenient way to do something will vary depending on context. Now you should use whatever methods feel right as your habits develop.

Putting Things onto a Floppy Disk

Copying a document (or a program for that matter) onto a floppy disk is as easy as copying to a folder or onto the Desktop.

Dragging an Icon to the Floppy Drive

This won't work if you don't have a floppy disk in your drive.

1 Put a disk in your floppy drive.

2 Double-click My Computer to open its window.

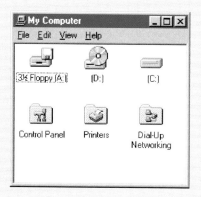

3 Click the Autumn Leaves icon on the Desktop and drag it up and onto the floppy drive icon in the My Computer window.

▶ The pointer automatically becomes a copy pointer (with the plus sign).

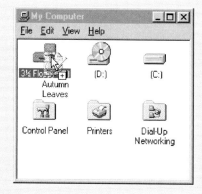

NOTE
Windows assumes that you want to keep your original document on the hard drive. Hold down Shift to override this and move the document.

4 Release the mouse button.

▶ A Copying dialog box appears on the screen with a cute little animation of a document flying from one file folder to another, apparently a page at a time.

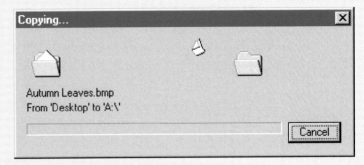

Sending an Icon to the Floppy Drive

There's an easier way to put things on a floppy that doesn't even require that you get the floppy drive icon onto the screen.

1 Close the My Computer window.

2 Right-click on the Autumn Leaves icon.

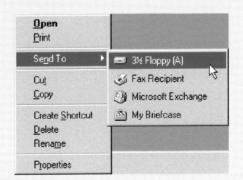

3 Select Send To ➤ 3½ Floppy (A).

4 When the Confirm File Replace dialog box appears (you just put a copy of this document on the floppy), click No.

What could be easier?

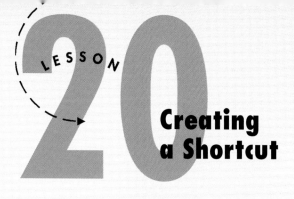

Creating a Shortcut

5 MINUTES

Shortcuts are probably the single most useful new feature of Windows 95. A shortcut is just a *pointer* to a program, document, or folder somewhere else on the computer. The benefit of shortcuts is that you can place these pointers anywhere, making your most important and useful programs, documents, and folders available from multiple locations, without having to take up disk storage space with duplicate copies of files. (While you *could* just make copies of programs and documents on your Desktop or in various common folders, you'd quickly run out of hard disk storage space.)

Of course, there are many ways to create shortcuts, and I'll run through the easiest in this lesson.

Pasting a Shortcut

One way to create a shortcut is a variation on the familiar copy and paste routine.

1 Click in the Windows window.

2 Scroll down through the window until the Notepad program icon comes into view.

3 Click the Notepad icon.

4 Select Edit ➤ Copy.

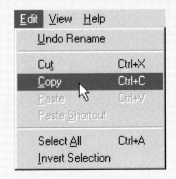

5 Now right-click on the Desktop a little to the right of the Autumn Leaves document icon.

▶ A menu pops up.

6 Select Paste Shortcut.

▶ A shortcut icon appears, named, appropriately enough, *Shortcut to Notepad.*

You can tell it's a shortcut by this little curling arrow on a white square.

7 Click the name and wait a moment for the name to become highlighted.

8 Then type a new name for the shortcut: Take a memo.

9 Press Enter.

Creating a Shortcut by Right-Clicking

The shortcut you just made points to a program, Notepad, but shortcuts can also point to documents. Create a document using your new shortcut.

1 Double-click the *Take a memo* shortcut.

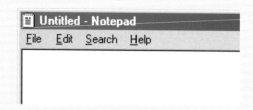

▶ The Notepad program starts up.

2 Type Don't forget to call accountant.

3 Select File ➤ Save.

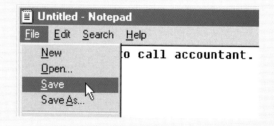

4 Click the Up One Level icon (to the right of the *Save in* box) in the Save As dialog box.

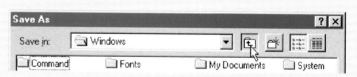

▶ The Save As dialog box now shows the contents of the hard drive (C:).

5 Double-click the Test folder.

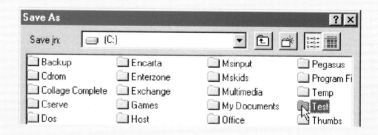

126

6 Type Don't forget! in the *File name* box.

7 Click Save.

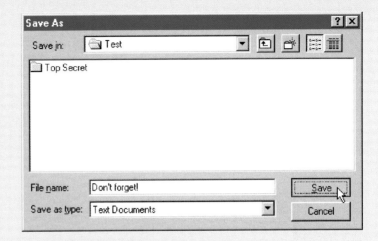

8 Click the Close button in the Notepad title bar.

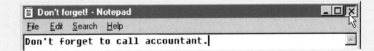

Right-Clicking

OK, that was a lot of preparation, but now you can make a shortcut to your new document.

1 Click the Test window.

127

2 Right-click the *Don't forget!* icon.

▶ A menu pops up.

3 Select Create Shortcut.

▶ A shortcut icon named *Shortcut to Don't forget!* appears in the Test window.

> **NOTE**
> Naturally, you wouldn't ever need a shortcut in the same folder as the thing it points to. Making a shortcut this way is generally a prelude to moving it elsewhere.

Right-Clicking and Dragging

The other way to use right-clicking is to right-click, drag, and then release (as you saw in Lesson 18).

1 Right-click the Don't forget! icon in the Test window and hold down the mouse button.

2 Drag down to the Desktop, somewhere between the Autumn Leaves document icon and the Take a memo shortcut icon.

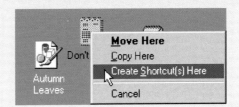

3 Release the mouse button.

4 Select Create Shortcut(s) Here from the menu that pops up.

▶ A shortcut appears, also named *Shortcut to Don't forget!*

5 Click the name and wait for it to become highlighted.

6 Select the text *Shortcut to.*

7 Press Delete.

8 Press Enter.

NOTE

Unless you want all your shortcuts to be named "Shortcut to *something or other*," get used to having to manually cut out the first part of the name. Of course, you can name your shortcuts whatever you want, as in the case of the *Take a memo* shortcut.

Creating a New Shortcut from Scratch

You can also create a shortcut on the spot and then assign it to a program, document, or folder. Folders are the trickiest, so I'll walk you through that procedure.

> **NOTE**
>
> It can be a great convenience to have a shortcut to a folder on your Desktop. If you have some folder buried several layers down in the hierarchy and you're forever working your way down to it, starting with My Computer, consider making a shortcut to that folder on your Desktop. Then you can instantly jump to the folder with a double-click of the mouse.

1 Right-click on the Desktop below the bottom-right corner of the Windows window.

▶ A menu pops up (will wonders never cease?).

2 Select New.

▶ The New submenu will appear on the left, because there isn't room for it to the right of the pop-up menu.

3 Select Shortcut.

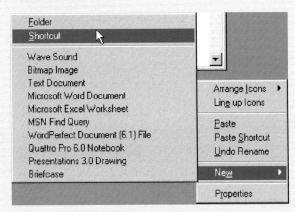

▶ The Create Shortcut dialog box will appear on the screen (and a New Shortcut icon with a generic Windows logo on it will appear where you clicked).

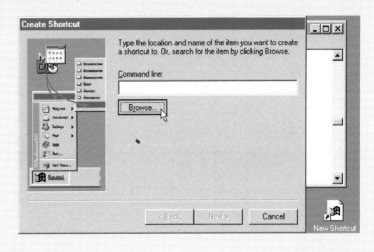

4 Click Browse. (You could also just go ahead and type the "path" leading to the folder you want, if you know it offhand; you'd then skip to step 12.)

▶ A Browse dialog box appears, looking much like a Save As or Open dialog box.

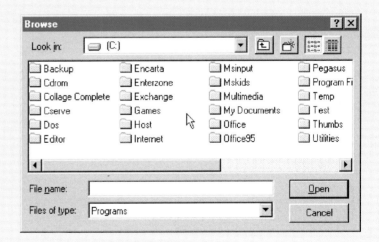

5 Double-click the Test folder.

6 Double-click the Top Secret icon.

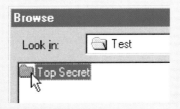

NOTE

Here's the tricky part of creating a new shortcut and assigning it to a folder: the Browse dialog box will only let you select programs and documents. The best you can do is to select a file name *in* the folder you want, and then edit the reference in the Create Shortcut dialog box.

No programs appear in the Top Secret folder (as there are none), so you have to turn the attention of the Browse dialog box to all files.

7 Click the *Files of type* drop-down list box and select All Files.

Files of type:	Programs ▼
	Programs
	All Files

8 Select Fall Leaves.

| File name: | Fall Leaves | | Open |
| Files of type: | All Files ▼ | | Cancel |

9 Click Open.

▶ You are returned to the Create Shortcut dialog box with the complete path to the Fall Leaves document now appearing in the *Command line* box.

Create Shortcut

Type the location and name of the item you want to create a shortcut to. Or, search for the item by clicking Browse.

Command line:

"C:\Test\Top Secret\Fall Leaves.bmp"

NOTE

If you were creating a shortcut to a program or document, you wouldn't have to bother with the next step.

10 Select the *Fall Leaves.bmp* portion of the command line.

Command line:

"C:\Test\Top Secret\Fall Leaves.bmp"

NOTE
Be careful not to select the quotation mark at the end of the command line.

11 Press Delete.

12 Click the Next button.

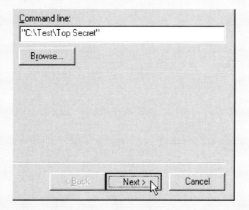

Command line:

"C:\Test\Top Secret"

Browse...

< Back   Next >   Cancel

▶ The dialog box then suggests a name for the shortcut, the actual name of the folder.

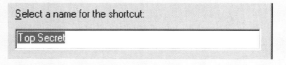

Select a name for the shortcut:

Top Secret

13 Click the Finish button.

< Back   Finish   Cancel

▶ The new shortcut icon gets the name Top Secret but still sports the generic Microsoft logo.

Top Secret

▶ After a moment, Windows figures out that the short-cut points to a folder and changes the symbol to a folder shortcut icon.

14 Click in the name, wait for it to become highlighted, and type Important.

15 Press Enter.

Try out your new folder shortcut. (Choose the Top Secret folder in the Taskbar if it's not currently visible.)

1 Drag the *Shortcut to Don't forget!* icon from the Test window onto the *Important* folder shortcut.

▶ The *Shortcut to Don't forget!* icon appears immediately in the Top Secret folder.

Copying Shortcuts

Shortcuts can be copied (as well as moved, dragged, etc.) just as any other icons can.

1 As one last bit of mischief, click just above and to the left of the Don't forget! shortcut icon on the Desktop and drag to create a ghost rectangle, growing down and to the right until it encompasses Take a memo and Important in addition to Don't forget! All the icons lassoed by the rectangle become highlighted.

2 Now press Ctrl+C to copy them all.

3 Press Ctrl+V to paste them.

Copies of all three—named, of course, *Copy of Don't forget!*, *Copy of Take a memo*, and *Copy of Important*—appear on the Desktop, but they're hard to see with so many windows open.

4 Close all the windows to reveal the current clutter of your Desktop. (Of course yours will not match mine exactly, but you should have the same icons floating around).

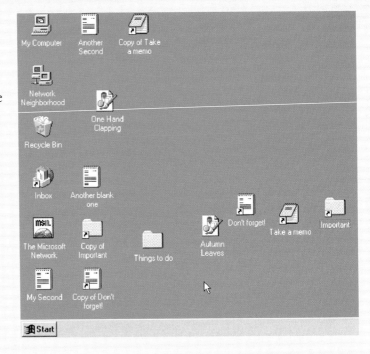

> **NOTE**
>
> That same method of lassoing icons and then copying them (or for that matter performing any other actions) will work for all types of icons, whether they're in windows or on the Desktop. Be careful, though, about accidentally creating many copies of multiple icons. Don't forget you can always undo an action on the Desktop.

5 MINUTES

Keeping the Desktop Neat

Now that you've started throwing a bunch of documents, copies of documents, and shortcuts on your Desktop, things are starting to get a bit cluttered up (not unlike a real desktop).

Windows provides a bunch of different ways of arranging or neatening up the icons on the Desktop (and the same set of options is available in any folder window).

Straightening Out the Icons on the Desktop

One drawback to most of the automatic icon-arranging commands is that they'll put your icons all in rows, starting from the upper-left part of the Desktop and working down one column at a time. There's nothing inherently wrong with this. If you start leaving icons, such as shortcuts, in specific places on your Desktop, though, in order to find them easily or drop other icons onto them, then you might not want to have everything packed over onto the left side of the screen.

One of the commands, fortunately, will neaten up the Desktop, moving jumbled icons to the nearest position on an invisible grid. Try this now.

1 Right-click on the Desktop.

2 Choose Line up Icons from the menu that pops up.

▶ The icons straighten themselves out. (Yours may settle
in slightly different positions, depending on where
you've actually been pointing while placing various
icons on the Desktop.)

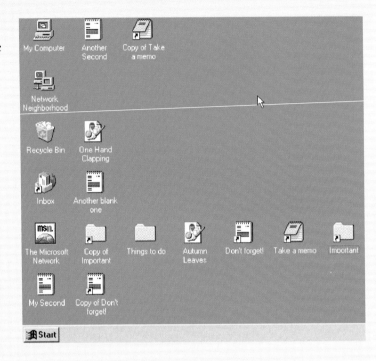

Organizing the Desktop

If you don't mind losing the rough positions of the icons, you can choose one of the
more heavy-duty Arrange Icons options to sort things out.

1 Right-click on the Desktop.

2 Select Arrange Icons.

3 Select *by Type*.

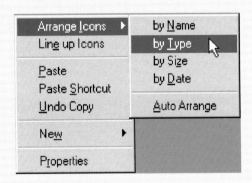

▶ The icons shuffle over to
the left side of the screen,
arranged in an overall order
that may only make sense
to the designers of Win-
dows, but grouped by type,
so all the Paint documents
come one after another, as
do all the shortcuts, and all
the Notepad documents.
(Shortcuts are treated as
shortcuts and not as the
type of file they point to.)

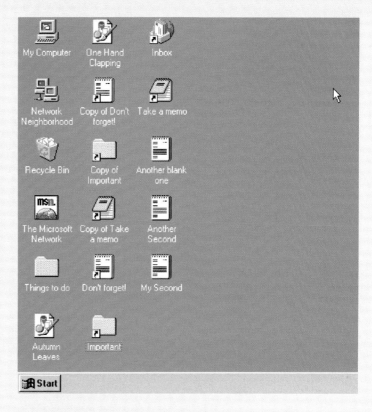

4 Right-click the Desktop
again.

5 Select Arrange Icons ➤ by
Date.

The icons then rearrange themselves again, this time in date order (meaning the order in which they were created), except for certain icons, such as My Computer. Although this command sometimes yields some odd or questionable results (such as putting some older icons after newer ones), it's generally a good way to sort things out if you're looking for files from a specific time period (such as recent documents).

Filing Documents Away in Folders

The Desktop really plays two distinct roles, both important. It serves as a permanent place for useful shortcuts, and as a handy temporary place for documents and other files in transition. The latter types of files, such as those copied from a floppy disk, downloaded from an online service, or created on the Desktop, generally need to be filed away at some point, lest your Desktop get too cluttered and stuffed with icons.

If you're in the midst of a project that involves a lot of documents or even a lot of notes jotted down, you might want to corral those stray documents every now and then and drop them all into a folder, just to keep them out of sight. You could put them in a folder on the Desktop or in a folder via a shortcut on the Desktop.

1 Click and drag a selection rectangle around the three Notepad documents *Another blank one, Another Second*, and *My Second*. (If they're not all conveniently in a row, select as many as you can at first.)

2 Hold down the Ctrl key.

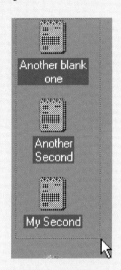

3 Click *Copy of Don't forget!* and *Copy of Take a memo* to add them to the selection. (If you were unable to select any of the three documents in step 1, use this method to select them now.)

4 Click on any of the selected icons and hold down the mouse button.

5 Drag the multiple selection to the *Things to do* folder. (If you have any trouble, such as accidentally un-selecting some of the icons, just go back to step 1 and start over.)

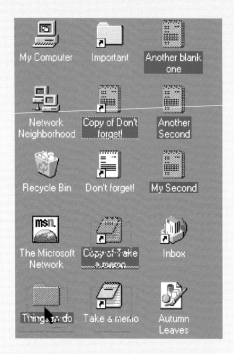

▶ The icons disappear, neatly filed away in the Things to do folder.

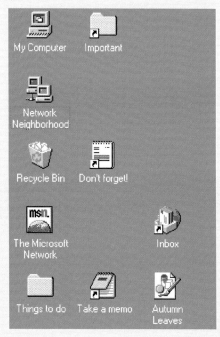

6 To reorganize the remaining icons, right-click the Desktop.

7 Select Arrange Icons ➤ Auto Arrange.

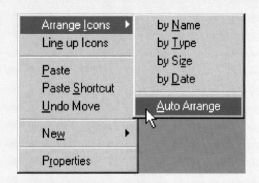

▶ The icons neaten themselves up into two columns only. While Auto Arrange is turned on, icons will automatically snap into place in neat columns.

8 Right-click the Desktop again.

9 Select Arrange Icons ➤ Auto Arrange (to turn off Auto Arrange). The icons stay still and you can add new icons or rearrange icons without them snapping to the grid automatically.

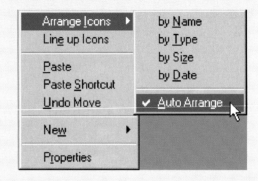

I hope these tricks help you keep your Desktop manageable.

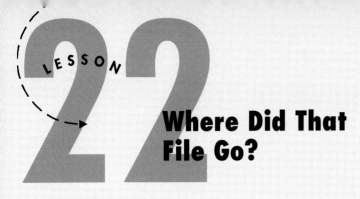

LESSON 22

Where Did That File Go?

5 MINUTES

If you've ever used a computer before, then you already know how easy it is to lose a document (usually an important one) somewhere on your computer. You *know* it's there, but you can't find it. It didn't help in the past that file names were often a random-seeming stream of letters and numbers.

But even documents with nice plain-English file names get lost. Sometimes you save a document without really looking where it's being saved. However it happens, those files get lost one way or another. Fortunately, Windows now has a very slick Find feature that not only makes it very easy to search for a file, even if you only know part of its name, but also works automatically when you try to run a program or open a document that's been moved.

Time to give Find a workout.

Finding a File

Say you're looking for that pesky Autumn Leaves image. Go back to where it all starts.

1 Click the Start button.

2 Select Find on the Start menu.

3 Select Files or Folders. (You may have only that one choice.)

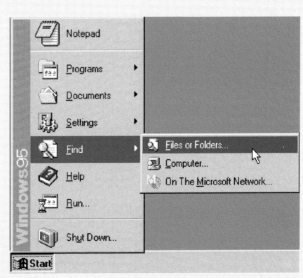

▶ This brings up the Find dialog box. Don't let its complicated looks fool you. It's perfectly easy. Most of the time, all you do is type a file name (or part of one) and press Enter (or click the Find Now button, which amounts to the same thing). The title bar says *All Files* because you haven't specified anything yet.

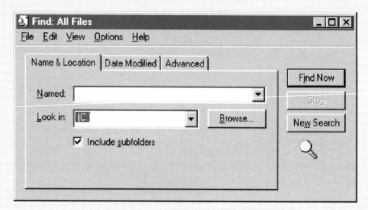

NOTE

The other tabs, the Look in box, the Browse button, the Include subfolders check box, and the menu options all give you some slight edge in very specific search situations, but you can ignore them most of the time.

4 Type leaves.

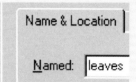

NOTE

If you want to type a file name that contains multiple words separated by spaces, then put the whole name in quotation marks. Windows will automatically match any file name that contains any of the words you type in the Named box.

5 Click Find Now (or press Enter).

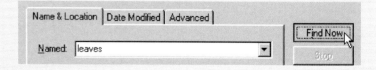

▶ A window appears at the bottom of the dialog box (it works exactly like the Details view of any folder window), and the magnifying glass starts revolving, occasionally tracing out the image of a dog-eared page. As Windows finds files with that word in their names, they start appearing in the window.

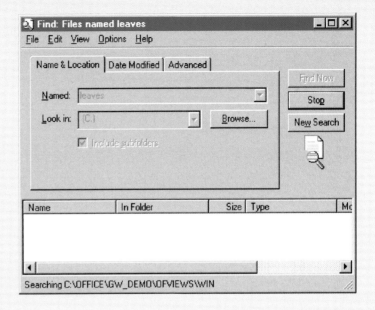

NOTE

Notice that the title bar has changed to identify the search. You can search for more than one file at once (just go back to the Start menu again and open another Find window), and it's nice to know which one is which, especially if they're minimized.

6 When the search is complete, scroll to the bottom of the list.

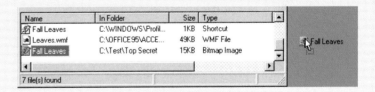

7 Right-click the Fall Leaves icon (the one in the Test\ Top Secret folder) and drag it rightward, onto the Desktop.

147

8 Release the mouse button.

▶ A menu pops up.

9 Choose Create Shortcut(s) Here.

NOTE

The window at the bottom of the Find dialog box is literally equivalent to a folder window. The icons in it are "live" in exactly the same way as the icons in a folder window, and you can do all the same things to them.

Saving a Search

Because a Find search creates an impromptu folder of sorts, you might find it useful to keep the results of the search around, for easy access to a certain group of files. Still, the next time you shut off your computer, at the latest, the results window from the search will be closed. To keep a windowful of search results around to use as a folder, you can save the search.

First you have to make sure that Find will save the results of your search (and not just the search criteria).

1 Select Options ➤ Save Results.

Now you can save the results.

2 Pull down the File menu.

3 Select Save Search.

▶ A new icon called *Files named leaves* appears on your Desktop. In the future, you can double-click that icon to gain quick access to this particular set of files.

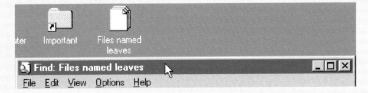

Searching for a Document by Its Contents

If you're really stuck, unable to find an important document because you can't remember its name, you can search for a word *in* the document. This takes much longer and you have to choose a word that's not too common, but most important documents have some particular language in them that you'll remember.

1 Click the New Search button.

▶ A dialog box appears warning you that you'll lose the results of the previous search.

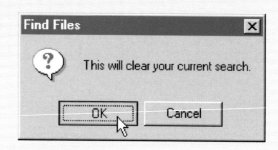

2 Click OK.

3 Click the Browse button.

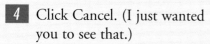

▶ The Browse for Folder dialog box appears, with a schematic of the hierarchy from the Desktop down to (C:) and other conceptual connections. You can click any of the little plus signs to have a next lower level expanded. So, clicking the hard drive (C:) would bring up all the folders you'd normally see in the (C:) window.

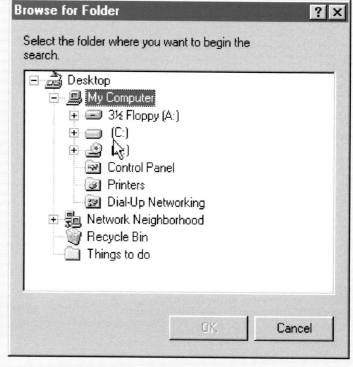

4 Click Cancel. (I just wanted you to see that.)

5 Click the Advanced tab in the Find dialog box.

▶ In the *Of type* box you can limit what kinds of files to search for to a specific document type or to folders.

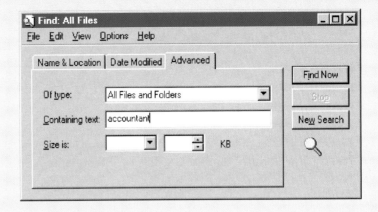

6 Type accountant in the *Containing text* box.

7 Click Find Now.

As Windows finds files that contain the word *accountant*, they appear in the window that opens up in the lower half of the dialog box, just as in any search.

8 After you've waited a little while, click the Stop button (it will go on for a long time if you let it).

9 Now close the Find dialog box.

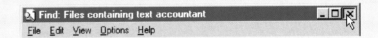

May you never lose anything again.

Throwing Stuff Away

5 MINUTES

One of the most satisfying things you can ever do with your computer is throw something away, delete it, "kill" it. (And one of the most frustrating is trying to recover something you threw away but didn't mean to. See Lesson 24 for more on that.) Naturally, there are scores of different ways to do this in Windows, but here are the quickest and easiest.

Dragging Things to the Recycle Bin

The purpose of the Recycle Bin icon on the Desktop is to give you a handy place to drag things to in order to throw them away.

1 Click the *Files named leaves* icon.

2 Drag it onto the Recycle Bin.

The icon disappears. See? Just as easy as dragging it into a folder.

Pressing the Delete Key

You can also use the Delete key to chuck a file. (It's a useful little key—good for text editing as well).

1 Click the *Shortcut to Fall Leaves* icon.

2 Press the Delete key.

3 Windows asks you to confirm that you want to throw away the file.

4 Click Yes.

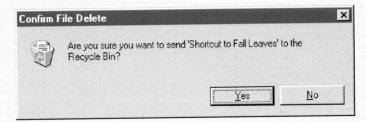

Deleting by Right-Clicking

Just to keep that right mouse button limber, try it that way as well.

1 Right-click the *Copy of Important* shortcut icon.

▶ A menu pops up.

2 Click Delete.

3 When asked to confirm the deletion, click Yes.

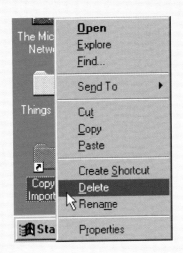

Deleting a Program

Windows has a nice failsafe built in for when you attempt to delete a program. (It's especially kind when you select a large number of files and attempt to delete them all at once—Windows will warn you of any program files lurking in the selection.)

First, make a copy of a program to be extra safe.

1 Open My Computer.

2 Open (C:).

3 Open Windows.

4 Scroll until Notepad comes into view.

5 Hold down Ctrl and drag a copy of the Notepad program onto the Desktop.

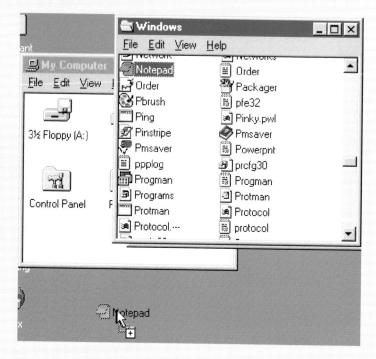

Now we'll use this copy of Notepad instead of the original.

6 Delete the Notepad copy on the Desktop (use whichever method you prefer).

▶ A special Confirm File Delete dialog box appears, warning you that if you delete a program file, you may later discover you can't run the program. In this case, you're deleting a copy, so it's OK.

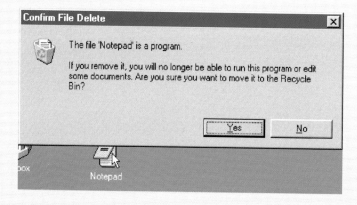

7 Click Yes.

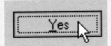

Deleting a Document You Created by Mistake

While saving a document, it's not uncommon to accidentally type the wrong name for the document, or to save the document in the wrong place. Because Open and Save As windows are "live" in the sense that the icons in them behave just as they do in Desktop windows, it's no problem to clean up after yourself when you make a little mistake like that.

Start a new document so you can see for yourself.

1 Double-click the *Take a memo* shortcut (or start the Notepad program any other way you prefer).

2 In the Notepad window, type Yet another random document.

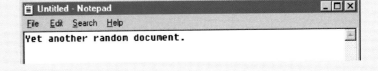

3 Select File ➤ Save.

4 Click the Up One Level button three times to aim the Save As dialog box at the Desktop.

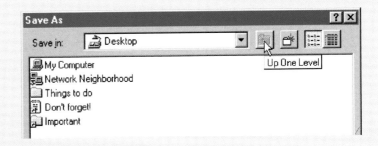

5 Type the following file name (with typo): **Not to myself**.

6 Click the Save button.

But wait! That's not the file name you meant to type, right? No problem, just return to the Save As dialog box.

1 Select File ➤ Save As.

2 Right-click the *Not to myself* icon.

▶ A menu pops up.

3 Click Delete.

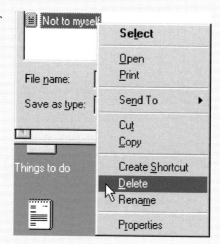

NOTE
You could also select the icon's name and change the file name directly, as long as it's in the right place. Normally, after deleting the incorrectly named file, you'd want to repeat the Save As process to save the document in the right place with the right name.

4 Click Cancel to close the Save As dialog box.

5 Exit Notepad. (Notice that it doesn't prompt you to save your document, although you deleted the only copy of it!)

6 Close the Windows window.

As you've seen, you can delete a file many different ways and in almost any context. And if you delete something by mistake? See Lesson 24 for what to do about it.

5 MINUTES

Oops! I Didn't Mean to Delete That!

Inevitably, you will delete a file that you meant to keep. Fortunately, deleting a file (or throwing it into the Recycle Bin, literally) does not purge the file from your disk. Actually, it just puts it in a category of doomed files and takes it out of normal circulation. The Find feature won't find deleted files, but they're still available to be undeleted until the Recycle Bin either is emptied or exceeds some maximum size and starts really deleting its oldest contents.

Undeleting Right Away

If you catch yourself immediately after mistakenly deleting a file, you can undo the deletion.

1 Drag the *Take a memo* icon to the Recycle Bin.

2 Right-click anywhere on the Desktop.

3 Choose Undo Delete from the menu that pops up.

NOTE

An even simpler shortcut for immediate recovery of deleted files is to press Ctrl+Z.

If you realize your mistake later, you're still in luck.

Opening the Recycle Bin

If you think you've thrown something away by mistake, what do you do? Rummage through the trash, of course.

1 Double-click the Recycle Bin.

▶ The Recycle Bin opens, looking like any normal folder window, in Details view. In this case, though, the details include the files' original locations and the dates they were deleted. You might have other files in your Recycle Bin if you've been doing some other deleting outside the scope of this book.

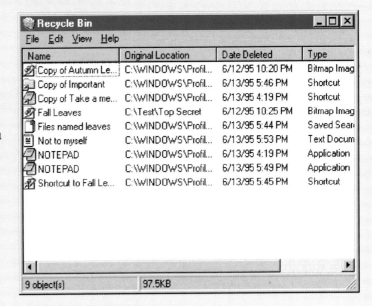

2 Click the *Not to myself* icon.

3 Drag it out of the Recycle Bin (you could also select File ➤ Restore to restore the deleted file to the folder it was deleted from).

▶ The document appears on the Desktop, safe and sound.

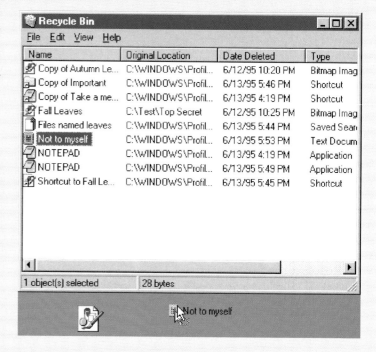

4 Click the name plate and wait for the name to become selected.

5 Move the insertion point to the end of the word *not*.

6 Type e and press Enter.

7 Close the Recycle Bin.

Makes the whole prospect of deleting files a little less scary, doesn't it?

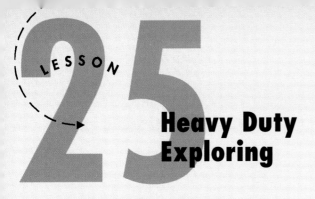

5 MINUTES

Heavy Duty Exploring

There is one other way to examine the contents of your computer, called the Windows Explorer, but you don't really need to know about it. I'll take you through a simple demonstration in this lesson, if you're interested. If you're not, just skip to the next lesson right away.

> **NOTE**
> The Explorer is based on the old File Manager in previous versions of Windows. If you've used Windows 3.1 or an earlier version, the Explorer might seem familiar to you.

Exploring by Right-Clicking

The easiest way to bring up the Explorer window is to right-click on an object on the Desktop or in a window. (You can't "explore" programs and documents, only folders, disk drives, and other special Windows objects.) Try this now.

1 Right-click on the My Computer icon.

▶ A menu pops up.

2 Select Explore.

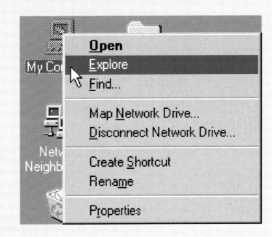

▶ A window appears entitled *Exploring - My Computer*. The window is split into two panes. The left side shows a tree structure illustrating the relationships among objects on your Desktop. The little plus symbols indicate further hidden layers of folders. The divider between the two panes can be clicked on and dragged to the left or right to change the relative size of the panes. The pane on the right shows the contents of the object you're exploring.

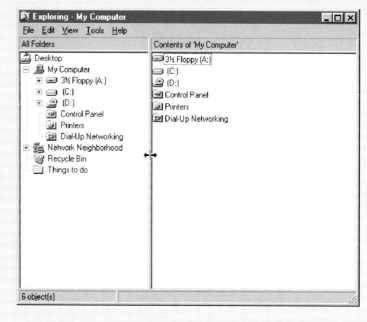

NOTE

Don't let it bother you that the title bar of the Explorer window says *Exploring* instead.

3 Click the plus sign next to the hard drive (C:) icon in the left pane.

▶ The tree in the left pane re-positions itself and expands below the (C:) icon to show all the folders directly on the hard drive. (Folders with subfolders also have the little plus signs).

4 Scroll, if necessary, down to the Windows folder and double-click it (not its plus sign).

▶ After taking a moment to think (that's what the hour-glass means), the Explorer changes the right pane to show the contents of the Windows folder. By now you may have noticed that, aside from the left pane, the Explorer window is not much different from any folder window on the Desktop. In fact, the icons in the window are "live" in exactly the same way they are in folder windows.

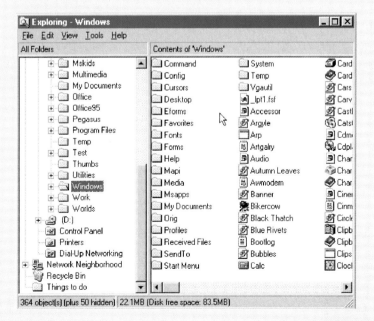

5 Press Backspace to go up one level to the hard drive (C:).

6 Close the Explorer window.

Starting with the Start Button

You can also start up the Windows Explorer from the Start menu.

1 Click the Start button.

2 Select Programs ➤ Windows Explorer.

▶ The Explorer window appears, aimed at the hard drive.

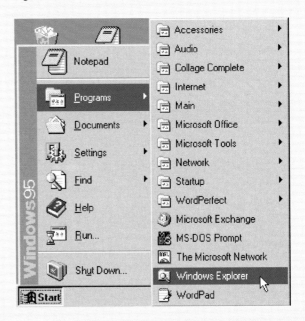

3 Close the window.

Exploring a Shortcut Folder

You can right-click on and explore a shortcut folder much like any other object on the Windows Desktop. Of course, you'll be shown the folder to which the shortcut points.

1 Right-click the Important shortcut folder.

▶ A menu pops up.

2 Select Explore.

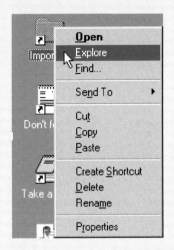

▶ The Explorer window appears, aimed at the Top Secret folder (that's the one that the Important shortcut points to).

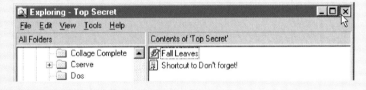

3 Close the Explorer window.

That wasn't too painful, was it? The final part of this book will deal with e-mail, networks, online services, and the Internet.

5

No Desktop Is an Island

Whether on a network or by modem, most computers are now connected to other computers and printers, at least some of the time. The modern office runs on electronic communication, and Windows 95 facilitates your connections to other people and resources. Besides covering e-mail and local networks, this part also shows you how to connect to the Microsoft Network, how to find your way around there, and how to explore the Internet from your Desktop via the World Wide Web.

5 MINUTES

Exchanging E-Mail

E-mail is rapidly becoming an essential part of office life (and computer use in general). If your computer is part of a network, then sending e-mail to your colleagues is simply a matter of running your e-mail program and dashing off a message. If you have dial-up access to a network, then things are a little trickier, but it's not really your job to make the underlying structure work. Your local guru should handle that.

There are a multitude of different e-mail systems, many of which can interact seamlessly. Windows 95 comes with a basic Microsoft Exchange package that can be used to send e-mail over a network as well as out over the Internet (assuming your office has a gateway to the Net). I'll demonstrate the use of Exchange as the e-mail program you're most likely to have. If your office has standardized with a different program, the look and feel might be different and some of the commands will be different, but the basic tasks will be the same.

> **NOTE**
>
> In this and some of the other lessons in this final part of the book, you won't be able to get exactly the same results as my screens will show. But you can still learn the basic steps by following along.

Running Your E-Mail Program

If Microsoft Exchange is set up on your computer, then you should have an Inbox icon on your Desktop. (It's really a shortcut to Exchange.) When you want to check for new mail (or if you've received an automated notice that you have new mail) or send a message, you start with this icon.

1 Double-click the Inbox icon.

Inbox

168

NOTE

If you've got a different e-mail program installed, you should be able to run it from the Start menu. The details will differ from the steps outlined in the rest of this lesson, but you can try to follow along as best as you can.

▶ First you'll see the welcome screen for Exchange. Just wait a moment as the program starts.

▶ Then the Exchange window will appear. If the window shows two different panes, then on the left is a folder tree that shows where different types of messages are stored.

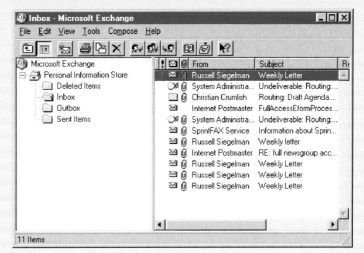

NOTE

Notice that the Inbox folder is open when you start. You can click the other folders to see deleted messages, messages you've written that haven't been delivered yet, and messages you've sent. Almost all the time, though, you'll want to work in the Inbox folder, so it's convenient that that's the one open when you start. On the right side are all the messages in your Inbox. (Messages with the paper clip icon have attached files.)

2 To switch to the single pane view, select View ➤ Folders (to uncheck Folders).

▶ There, now you can see your messages and all the information about them more easily (of course your messages, if any, will differ from mine). Those buttons at the top of each column can be used to sort the messages.

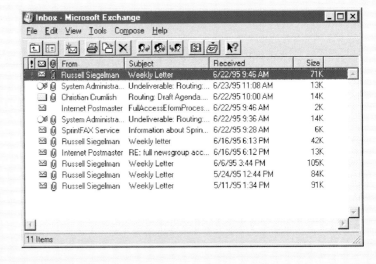

3 Click the From button to sort your messages by sender. (By default, they're sorted in the order received).

The toolbar at the top of the window has buttons for the most common actions you might want to perform.

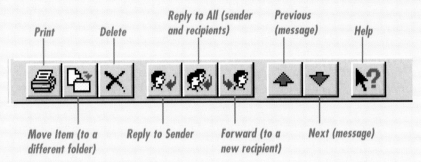

Reading a Message

The two main things you do with e-mail are read messages and send messages. Often you'll send messages in response to a received message, so most often you read your incoming messages first, then compose replies, and finally send out new messages, if any.

1 To read a message, double-click it in the Inbox listing.

▶ A new window appears, with the subject of the message in the title bar. The top area of the window shows who sent you the message, when it was sent, the recipient(s), and the subject. The window area contains the contents of the message. For longer messages, scroll or press Page Down to read the parts of the message not currently on the screen.

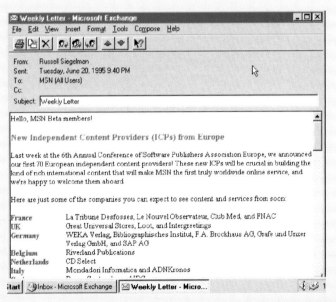

Replying to a Message

More than half of the e-mail messages you send will be in response to messages you've received.

1   Click the Reply to Sender button to reply to the sender of a message.

2   Type a reply. (You might want to erase any portion of the original message that's not relevant to the reply to make it easier for your correspondent to see the context of your reply.)

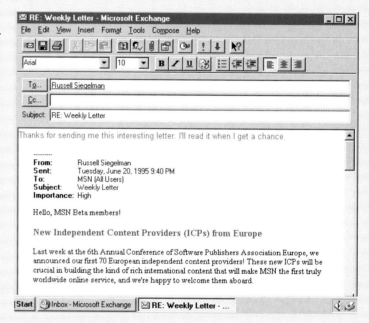

3   Select File ➤ Send to send the message. (You could also click the first button on the toolbar—the one that looks like an envelope—or press Ctrl+Enter).

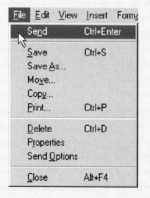

Sending a New Message

You don't have to reply to a previous message in order to send one.

1 To send a message, select Compose ➤ New Message.

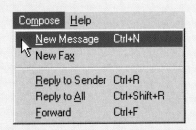

▶ A new window appears, with blank spaces for the recipient(s) and the subject.

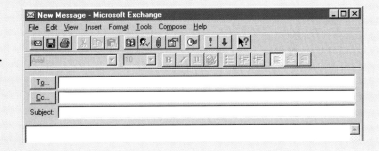

2 Click the To button.

▶ This opens up your address book. It contains all the e-mail addresses you know. It may be filled with addresses already (put there by whoever set up your e-mail system), or you may have to enter recipients into your address book the first time you send each one a message.

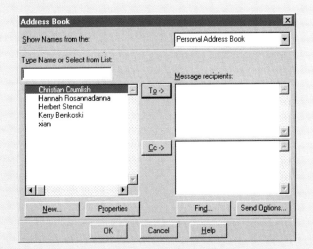

173

3 Select a recipient and click the To button.

4 Click OK.

5 Click in the Subject box and type a subject. (Keep it short but descriptive.)

6 Press Tab.

7 Type your message.

> **NOTE**
> To add a recipient, click the New button and follow the instructions.

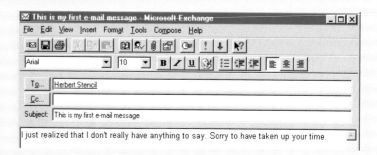

8 When you're done writing (and proofreading!) your message, click the Send button.

Exiting Exchange

Once you've read all your new messages, replied to any that require it, and sent out any new messages of your own, you're done and you can quit Microsoft Exchange.

1 Select File ➤ Exit.

▶ Exchange will send out all the messages you've composed and then disappear from the screen.

There, now you have yet another avenue for office gossip.

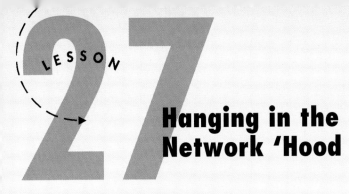

10 MINUTES

Hanging in the Network 'Hood

If your computer is on a network, then Windows 95 makes it just about as easy to use the resources of the other computers on the network as it is to open folders and run programs from your own hard disk. (If your computer is not on a network, skip this lesson.)

Opening a Document on Another Computer

The Network Neighborhood icon on your Desktop gives you access to documents, programs, and folders across your network similar to the kind of access you enjoy to your computer via the My Computer icon.

Rooting Around on the Network

To hunt around the network for a specific document, start from the Network Neighborhood icon.

1 Double-click the Network Neighborhood icon.

▶ The Network Neighborhood window opens, showing you each of the computers on the network (along with an icon that represents the network as a whole).

NOTE

Naturally, the computers on your network will have different names from the ones shown here, and there will most likely be a different number of computers as well.

2 Double-click the computer you want to look around on.

▶ A computer window opens showing the resources on the computer you chose.

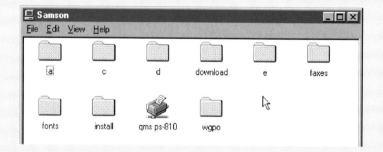

3 Double-click the drive you want to look on (over the network, all the drives look like folders).

4 Scroll through the window, if necessary.

5 Open additional folders, if necessary.

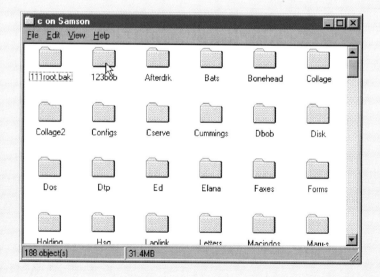

176

6 Double-click the document you want to open.

▶ The document opens as a normal document would.

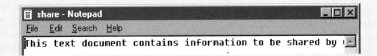

Saving a Local Copy of a Document

If you want to make a copy of a document and save it on your own computer (don't do this if you need to synchronize your changes with other people's), save the document the normal way:

1 Select File ➤ Save As.

▶ The Save As dialog box appears.

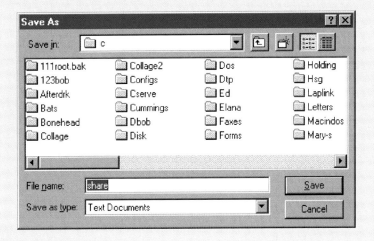

2 Click the *Save in* area and choose a drive on your own computer. (Some programs will still use a Windows 3.1-style dialog box, where you choose a drive at the bottom.)

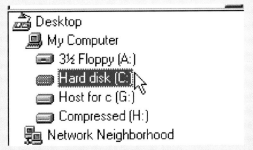

3 Choose a folder, if
necessary.

4 Click the Save button.

5 When you're done, close the
program window.

Opening a Document from within a Program

You can also run a program the normal way and then open a document from across
the network.

1 Start the Notepad program.

2 Select File ➤ Open.

3 Click the *Look in* drop-
down list box.

4 Choose the Network
Neighborhood icon.

5 Choose the computer on the network you want to look in.

6 Select the document you want to open, the same way you would from your own computer.

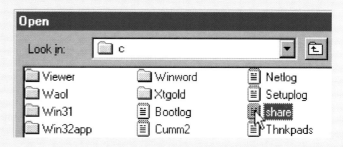

▶ The document opens.

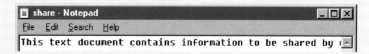

When you're done, quit the program as normal.

Treating a Network Drive as a Local Drive

If there's a drive out there on the network that you regularly want access to, you can *map* it, which means assigning it a letter (analogous to your C: drive). Then you can get access to it directly, without constantly rooting through the network hierarchy.

Mapping a Network Drive

Mapping a network drive is fairly simple. You start with the Network Neighborhood icon on your desktop.

1 Right-click the Network
Neighborhood icon.

2 Select Map Network
Drive from the menu that
pops up.

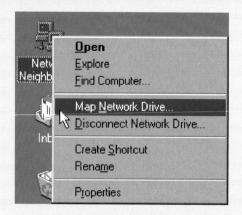

▶ The Map Network Drive
dialog box appears, with the
next available drive letter
suggested in the Drive box.

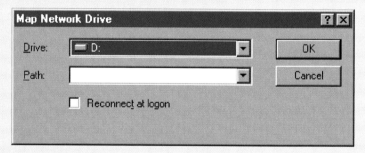

3 Click the Path box and
choose a drive from the list
that drops down. (Don't
worry about the funny dou-
ble backslash before the
other computer names.)

D:

\\DELILAH\DOWNLOAD
\\DELILAH\DRIVE C
\\SAMSON\C
\\SAMSON\D
\\SAMSON\E
\\SAMSON\WGPO

4 If you want this drive
mapped every time you
start your computer, check
the _Reconnect at logon_
option.

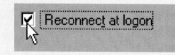

5 Click OK.

180

6 To see the results of your mapping, double-click the My Computer icon.

▶ The My Computer window opens with your mapped drive now appearing as one of the options (notice that the drive icon has a network "node" symbol attached).

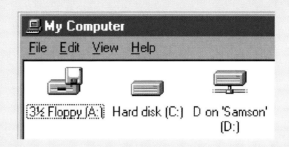

7 Double-click the mapped drive.

8 A window opens, showing the contents of the mapped drive.

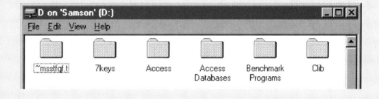

9 Close all windows.

Disconnecting a Network Drive

If you no longer need ready access to a mapped drive, you can disconnect it even more easily.

1 Right-click the Network Neighborhood icon.

2 Select Disconnect Network Drive.

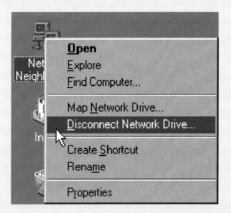

▶ The Disconnect Network Drive dialog box appears, showing all currently mapped network drives.

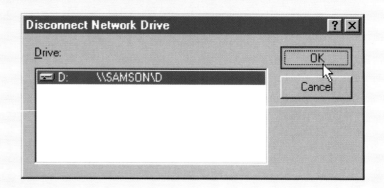

3 Select the drive to disconnect, if necessary.

4 Click OK.

Finding a Program or Document on Another Computer

So, you know how to hunt around the network for a specific document. But what if you're not really sure exactly where it is? Do you have to look in every nook and cranny of every computer on the network? Of course not. You can use the Find command instead.

1 Select Start ➤ Find ➤ Files or Folders.

2 When the Find dialog box appears, click the Browse button.

▶ The Browse for Folder dialog box appears, showing you the overall scheme of your computer.

3 Click the plus sign next to the Network Neighborhood icon.

4 Either click the Entire Network icon to search the network as a whole, or click one of the computers on the network if you are able to narrow down the search a little.

5 Click OK.

6 Type the salient portion of the file name you're searching for in the Named box.

7 Then click the Find Now button.

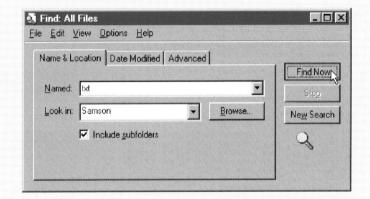

8 Scroll through the results window for the document you're looking for.

9 Double-click the document.

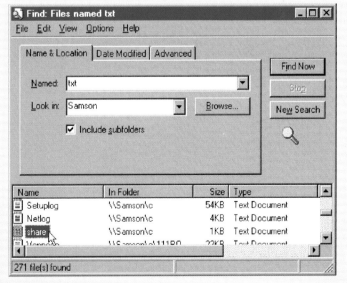

Printing Over a Network

One of the advantages of a network is that printers attached to it are available to everyone on the network. When you want to print a document, you can send it to a printer on the network as easily as to one attached to your computer. Printing in general is explained in Lesson 14.

Here's how to print over a network:

1 From within a program, select File ➤ Print (don't click the Print button!).

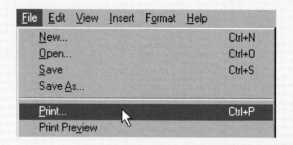

2 In the Print dialog box that appears, click the Name box and choose the network printer you want to print to.

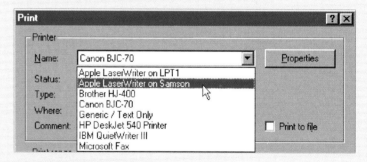

▶ A dialog box will appear telling you that your document is being printed on the network printer you chose.

Then walk over to the other printer and check to see if it's come out. Of course, since the network printer is by definition shared with other people, you might have to wait in a queue for your document to print. To see the status of the printer, double-click the printer icon at the right side of your Taskbar. (If there's no printer there, then your document is done.) A printer window will appear showing all the documents waiting to be printed, in order. While you can go ahead and move your document up in the queue, only do so if it's urgent. (Consult your network administrator for such policies.)

Joining the Microsoft Network

10 MINUTES

Windows 95 comes with built-in access to the new Microsoft Network, an online service (similar to America Online, Prodigy, CompuServe, and so on), with direct access to the Internet. You can sign up and try out the network for a month: the first ten hours are free, and each additional hour costs $2.50. After 30 days, you are automatically enrolled in the Standard Plan, which costs $4.95 a month and gives you three free hours every month (each additional hour is $2.50). If you don't want to be enrolled in the Microsoft Network after the 30-day trial period, you must cancel your membership. You'll need a valid credit card to sign up for your trial account.

Starting the Sign-Up for MSN

The Microsoft Network icon reads *Sign Up for The Microsoft Network* until you or someone else signs up. The first time you double-click it, it enables you to sign up. After you have successfully joined, the icon just reads *The Microsoft Network* and double-clicking it connects you to the network.

> **NOTE**
> If the icon just says The Microsoft Network, click Start ➤ Run, type signup, and press Enter. The MSN sign-up program will start.

1 Double-click the Sign Up for The Microsoft Network icon.

▶ The first dialog box that appears displays mostly promotional material.

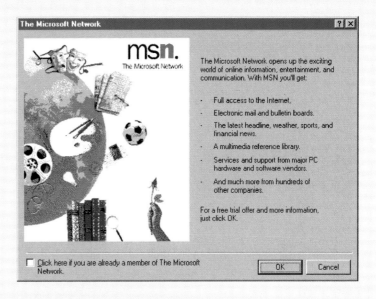

2 Click OK.

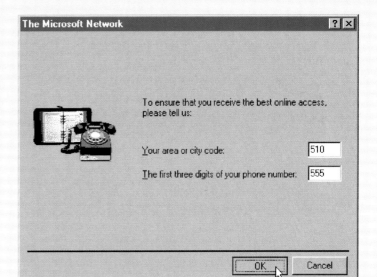

▶ Windows knows what your area code is.

3 Correct the area code if it's wrong.

4 Type the first three letters of your phone number.

5 Click OK.

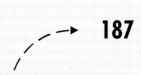

▶ The signup program tells you what numbers it's going to use to dial up the network. (You may have a different number of boxes than I do.)

6 Click Connect.

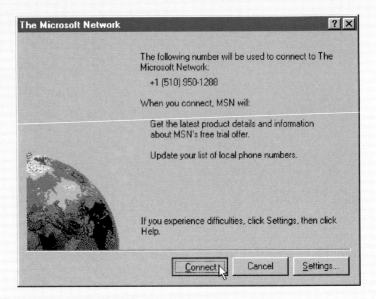

▶ The program tells you that it's dialing.

▶ Down on the right end of the Taskbar, a modem icon will show you the outgoing (left) and incoming (right) traffic. Green means that data is transmitting. Red means nothing is happening. You'll also have an MSN icon down there whenever you're connected to the Microsoft Network.

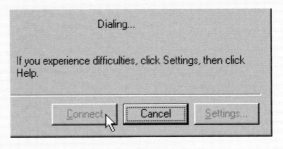

Jumping through a Few Hoops

Before you sign up as a member, the Microsoft Network wants you to understand what you're getting into.

▶ Before you can join the Microsoft Network, you have to give your name and address, enter a credit card number, and read the rules of the network. It's also a good idea to read the details and the price information first.

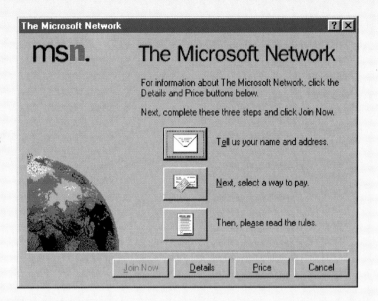

What You'll Find on the Network

Read about the contents of the Microsoft Network.

1 Click the Details button.

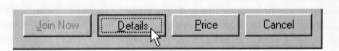

▶ The program displays a box with information about what's available on MSN.

2 Scroll through the box to read the whole thing.

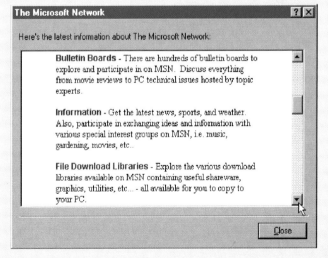

3 Click Close.

Pricing Information

Find out what the Microsoft Network costs.

4 Click the Price button.

▶ The program displays pricing information. (At the time this screen was captured, the Microsoft Network was still in beta and was therefore free.)

5 Click Close.

Your Name and Address

Enter your name and address.

6 Click the *Tell us your name and address* button.

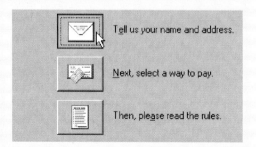

190

▶ A blank name, address, and phone number form appears.

7 Fill it out.

8 Click OK.

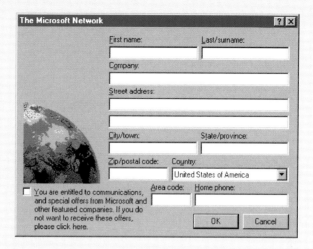

Choosing a Payment Method

Now get your credit card out.

9 Click the *Next, select a way to pay* button. (Notice the big check mark next to the completed step above.)

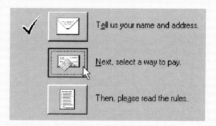

▶ A credit card form appears.

10 Choose a credit card type.

11 Fill out the form.

12 Click OK.

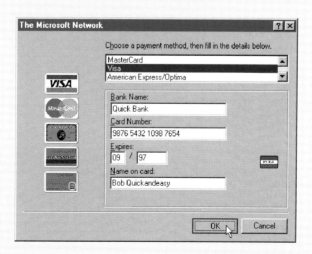

Read the Rules of the Road

Read up on the guidelines for correct behavior online with the Microsoft Network.

13 Click the *Then, please read the rules* button.

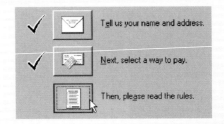

▶ Another box full of information (legalese, this time) will appear.

14 Scroll through the box to read it all.

15 Click the I Agree button.

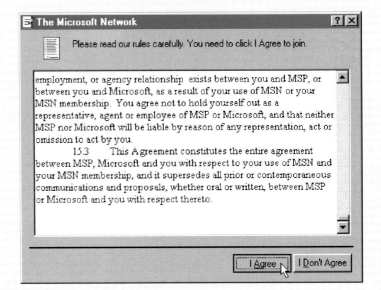

Joining MSN

Now (finally!), you're ready to join the Microsoft Network.

1 Click the Join Now button.

▶ The program displays two access numbers (your primary number, and a backup in case the first one's busy).

2 Click OK.

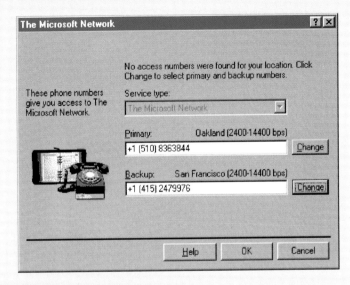

▶ You're back at another one of those Calling dialog boxes.

3 Click Connect.

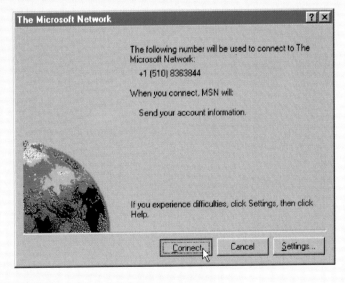

▶ The program tells you it's dialing (again).

▶ You've reached the final hurdle. Time to choose a Member ID and a password. If the ID (or *username*) you want is already taken, MSN will tell you and request that you choose another. Make sure your password is long and impossible to guess.

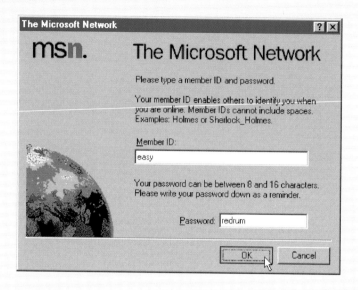

4 Type a Member ID.

5 Press Tab.

6 Type a password.

7 Click OK.

▶ A last dialog box appears, mainly just to let you know that your membership is fully set up.

8 Click Finish.

To go ahead and sample the Microsoft Network, continue on to the next lesson.

Sampling the Microsoft Network

15 MINUTES

Once you've signed up for the Microsoft Network (or MSN, or msn, as it's often called), go ahead and make your first visit. I'll show you around.

NOTE

The Microsoft Network is changing all the time, with new services being added and the appearance of various areas being upgraded. Don't worry if the environs don't match my screens exactly. The gist will be the same.

Signing In to MSN

Every time you connect to the Microsoft Network, you have to sign in.

1 Double-click the Microsoft Network icon on your Desktop.

▶ The Sign In dialog box appears.

2 Make sure your Member ID is correct.

3 Press Tab.

4 Type your password.

5 Check *Remember my password* (unless you're concerned, for security reasons, that someone might attempt to sign in to your MSN account from your computer).

6 Click the Connect button.

Several windows will appear after your computer connects with MSN.

> **NOTE**
> The order that these various dialog boxes pop up may vary for you. Don't worry about that. Also, you may have a different e-mail program.

First you'll see MSN Central.

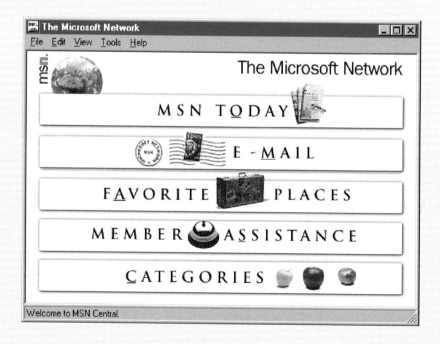

Click on any of the big bars to explore an area of MSN. We'll get to that in a moment. Then MSN Today, a daily broadsheet with announcements of high-profile events appears.

The illustrations and highlighted text are clickable links that take you directly to the event being advertised.

▶ Finally, Windows will check to see if you've received any new mail via your MSN account.

Checking Your Mail

If you have new mail, MSN will alert you. (If not, you can skip ahead to *Exploring MSN by Categories*, and go over this section when you *do* get mail.)

▶ MSN tells you that you've received new mail.

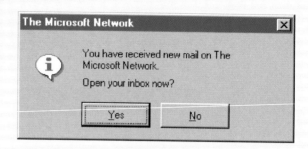

1 Click Yes.

▶ Microsoft Exchange will start up, unless you have some other e-mail program configured to cooperate with MSN. If you use some other e-mail program, then you'll only be able to follow the rest of this section very loosely.

▶ Next, your Inbox in Microsoft Exchange will open. (For more about e-mail and Exchange, see Lesson 26.) New messages will be listed in the right-hand pane in boldface.

2 To read a message, double-click it.

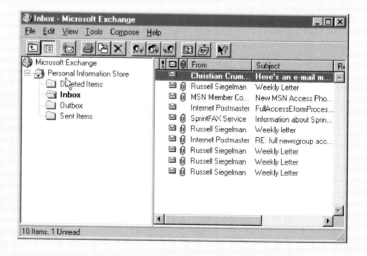

▶ The message will appear in a new window.

3 Read it.

4 To reply to it, choose an option from the Compose menu or click the Reply, Reply All, or Forward button on the toolbar.

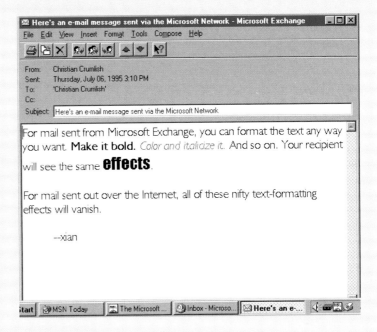

5 Click the Close button when you're done.

6 Then close the Microsoft Exchange button too, unless you have other e-mail business to attend to.

7 For that matter, close the MSN Today window as well (*not* the MSN Central window).

NOTE

If you close all the MSN windows, MSN will ask you if you want to sign out. To stay connected, click No.

Exploring MSN by Categories

The easiest way to visit an area of MSN devoted to some interest is to choose Categories from the MSN Central window. Once you find a topic you're interested in, you can look for information or programs, or join an ongoing conversation or a live one (these are written conversations I'm talking about, what MSN calls *BBSs* and *chat rooms*).

1 To start off, click the Categories bar in the MSN Central window.

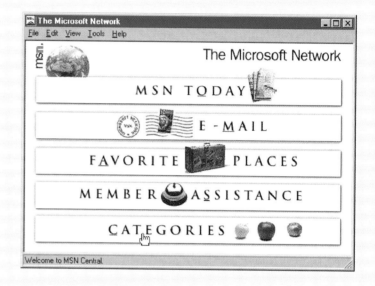

The Categories window will appear, replacing the MSN Central window. If you'd rather have each new subtopic open up in a separate window, select View ➤ Options, and in the Folder tab select *Browse folders using a separate window for each folder.*

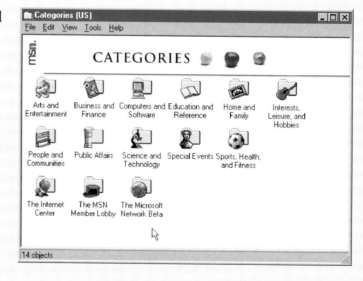

NOTE

You can use Backspace to work your way up category levels just as you would with windows representing folders on your own computer.

2 Double-click a category folder, such as Arts and Entertainment.

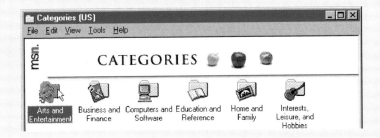

3 Then click a subcategory, such as *Movies*. (The subcategories may change, usually increasing in number, from time to time. Your choices may differ from the ones shown here.)

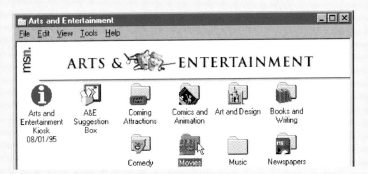

The subcategory window will appear, sometimes with its own special banner. There can be further subcategories within categories. The icons in one of these windows can represent a document to be downloaded (such as Kiosks with the international information *i* in a circle symbol), a BBS (with a bulletin board icon), a chat room (with a word balloon), a folder (which is like any other folder—it can hold other BBSs, chat rooms, files, and so on) a shortcut to another part of MSN, or other miscellaneous programs and information.

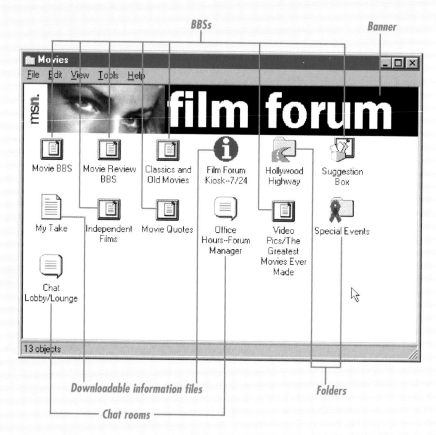

Catching Up with a BBS

A BBS (Bulletin Board System) traditionally refers to a small-time dial-up online service where members can usually get e-mail accounts and the opportunity to participate in ongoing discussions, posted in areas (also, confusingly, sometimes called bulletin boards) or live chats. On MSN, a BBS is just a place where public messages are posted, and the conversations take place over an extended period of time, not live.

1 To enter a BBS, double-click its icon (such as the Movie BBS icon).

▶ The BBS window will appear. BBSs contain messages (and can also have folders leading to subtopics). Messages are often part of ongoing conversations (strings of linked messages, usually under the same Subject heading). A message with a plus sign in a box to its left has replies hidden beneath it. A message with a paper clip contains an attachment (it can be a file or a shortcut to a location or document on MSN or the Internet).

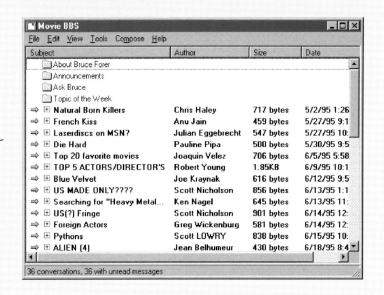

2 To see all the messages in a conversation, click the little plus sign.

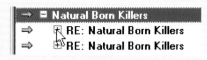

3 To have all the conversations in the BBS displayed, select View ➤ Expand All Conversations. It will take a few moments to sort things out and you may lose sight of whichever message you last highlighted. (Use the scroll bars to find your place again.)

Reading and Replying to Messages

Choose the first message you want to read by scrolling through the Subject lines.

1 To read a message, double-click it.

▶ It will appear in its own window, not unlike an e-mail message.

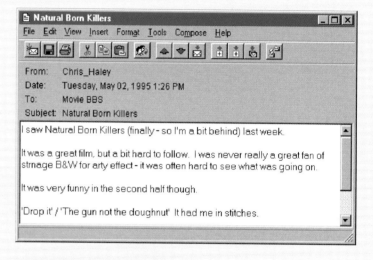

2 If you want to respond to the message, select Compose ➤ Reply to BBS. If you want to reply but not publically (usually a good idea for everyday chatter), select Compose ➤ Reply by E-mail. To send a copy of the message to someone else, select Compose ➤ Forward by E-mail. To post a new message to the BBS without reference to the current one, select Compose ➤ New Message.

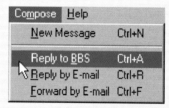

NOTE

Before you respond to a BBS message, stop and think it through first. If you're new to the conversation, read on to make sure someone else hasn't already put in your two cents.

▶ Whichever you choose, you'll be given a new message window.

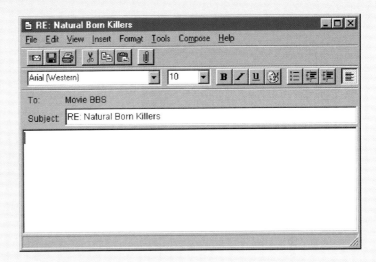

3 Type your message, formatting it with the menu or toolbar options, if you like.

4 When you're done, click the Send button to send your message.

You can read the next message in a conversation by choosing the Next Message button in the message's toolbar (it shows a large downward pointing arrow). You can also switch back to the BBS window to choose a different message or conversation to read.

5 Each message opens in its own window, so close the message you were reading when you're done with it, to keep them from stacking up.

Adding a BBS to Your Favorite Places

To save you from hunting around among categories all the time, MSN lets you put
shortcuts to any part of the network in a special folder called Favorite Places.

1 To add a BBS you like to
Favorite Places, select File
➤ Add to Favorite Places.

2 Close the BBS window
when you're done.

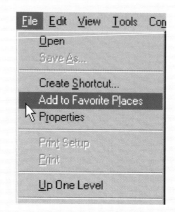

NOTE

You can add any category or folder window in MSN to your Favorite Places the same
way, from the File menu.

Joining a Chat

If you're in the mood for a "live" written conversation among any number of people,
all signed in at the same time, then you should visit a chat room. From the BBS window, hit Backspace to return to the Categories window.

1 To enter a chat, double-
click its icon (such as the
Film Chat icon).

Film Chat

The chat window will appear. It has three areas. The largest area in the upper left shows the on-going conversation, identifying each participant. You can scroll back to see earlier parts of the conversation. The small area at the bottom left is where you enter your contributions to the conversation. The area on the right shows all the people currently "in the room." (It is also possible to watch a chat without participating.)

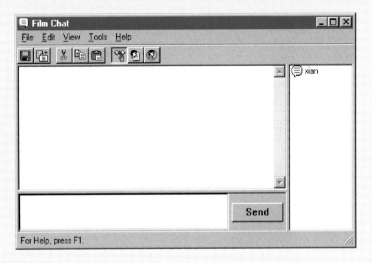

Speak Up

2 To join the chat, announce yourself (you can just jump right in and respond to someone's else's words, but that can seem brusque).

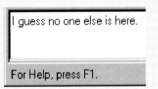

3 Press Enter.

4 Your words will appear below your Member ID in the upper area.

Adding a Chat Room to Your Favorite Places

5 To add a chat room to your Favorite Places, click the Add to Favorites icon in the toolbar.

To leave a chat, just close the window (say goodbye first!).

Checking Out the Internet

Lesson 30 will tell you more about the Internet, specifically browsing the World Wide Web with MSN's Internet Explorer or an alternative browser, such as Netscape Navigator. Many of the Internet's resources are available within MSN's normal structure, in the Internet Center.

Hit Backspace twice to get to the Categories window (from the Movies window).

1 Double-click the icon labeled *The Internet Center*.

▶ The Internet Center window appears, featuring informative documents, BBSs and chats like any other category, and folders leading to Usenet newsgroups (the popular forums accessible via the Internet).

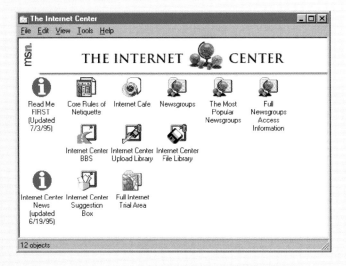

NOTE
The features in the Internet Center window will change, and will eventually include short-cuts to file archives, Gopher sites (menu-based tables of contents for the Internet), World Wide Web pages, and more.

Exploring Basic Netiquette

Before plunging onto the Internet, it would behoove you to learn the traditions of behavior and interaction that have made that international network of networks the most popular draw in cyberspace. (If you're already net-savvy, skip to the next section.) These guidelines are commonly referred to as *netiquette*. MSN offers a short summary.

2 Double-click the Core Rules of Netiquette icon.

▶ The rules appear. More information is available in newsgroups news.announce.newusers, and news.newusers.questions (we'll get to that soon). In general, work your way through the Internet slowly, take your time before joining ongoing conversations, and ask advice whenever your unsure about what to do.

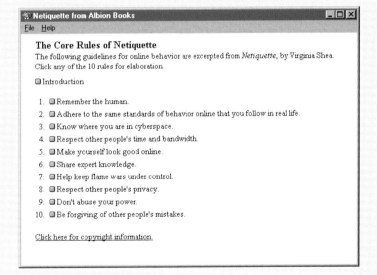

3 Close the window.

Reading Usenet Newsgroups

Usenet is a system of international discussion groups, called *newsgroups*. MSN gives you access to these groups via its BBS software. From your point of view, they might as well be Microsoft Network BBSs (but they're not! and people will complain if you refer to them that way).

1 To start exploring Usenet, double-click the icon labeled *The Most Popular Newsgroups*.

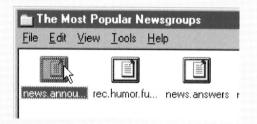

2 In the Most Popular Newsgroups window, double-click the news.announce. newusers BBS-style icon.

3 Then choose a conversation or message and start reading, as explained in *Catching Up with a BBS*, earlier in this lesson.

Close the window when you're done.

Visiting Your Favorite Places

I've shown you how to put BBSs, chat rooms, and other things in your Favorite Places, but not how to go there directly. Return to MSN Central (hit Backspace till you're there).

1 Click the Favorite Places bar.

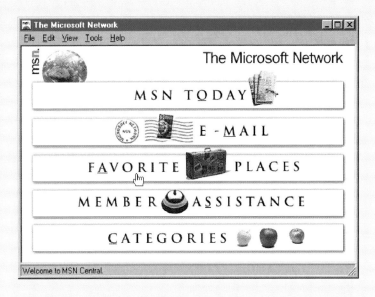

▶ The Favorite Places window appears, with direct short-cuts to all the places and things you've put there.

2 Double-click whichever feature you want to visit.

Getting Help and Advice

If you get confused or if things don't work the way they should, you can always get online help with MSN. Again, return to MSN Central.

1 Click the Member Assistance bar.

▶ The Member Assistance window appears, with all sorts of information and areas to ask questions.

2 Double-click any icon you like for information.

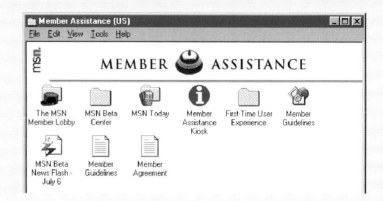

The MSN Icon in the Status Bar

As long as you're connected to MSN, a miniature MSN icon will appear in the right side of the Status bar. You can right-click it at any time to get a short menu of MSN options. This is especially useful when you've closed all the MSN windows without signing out.

1 Right-click the little MSN icon in the Status Bar.

2 Select the option you want.

Signing Out

When you've had your fill of the online service, it's time to sign out. You can sign out from any window's file menu.

1 Select File ➤ Sign Out.

NOTE

You can also right-click the little MSN icon in the Status Bar and select Sign Out.

▶ MSN will ask you to verify that you want to sign out.

2 Click Yes.

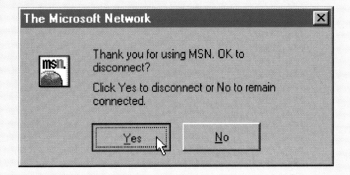

The Microsoft Network

Thank you for using MSN. OK to disconnect?

Click Yes to disconnect or No to remain connected.

Yes   No

213

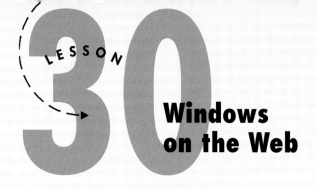

Windows on the Web

15 MINUTES

Nothing has popularized the Internet more effectively than the World Wide Web. Programs designed to browse the Web take almost all of the laborious details of Internet addressing and communications out of your hands, allowing you, for the mostpart, to simply point to topics of interest and click. Windows 95 does not automatically create Internet and Web access for you, but it helps the necessary tools function together smoothly.

If you have a Microsoft Network account, then you have full Internet access through it. Even without MSN, you may have access via a direct network connection from your office or school, or you may have some sort of dial-up access.

> **NOTE**
> See Lesson 28 for how to sign up for membership in the Microsoft Network.

With a network connection, you should simply be able to run any Web browser with no special preparation. With a dial-up account, you may need help from your service provider to configure everything properly. This lesson demonstrates the Web access provided with MSN and the Microsoft Internet Explorer (which comes with the Plus! Pack), as well as the use of an alternative Web browser, using the popular Netscape Navigator as an example.

MSN Shortcuts to the Web

Peppered throughout MSN are icons that represent shortcuts to resources on the Internet. All of them have a sort of web or latticework pattern in the background. Shortcuts to the Web automatically bring up the Internet Explorer and take you directly to a Web site.

1 Log in to the Microsoft Network (as explained in Lesson 29).

2 When you see an Internet shortcut (such as The Dilbert Zone, shown here— all Internet shortcuts have that same grid/spiderweb motif in their icons) you'd like to visit, double-click it.

▶ Windows downloads the address and starts up the Internet Explorer.

3 Maximize the window if it comes up not maximized.

▶ There, now you're out cruising the World Wide Web. Words in blue (gener-ally—or sometimes a differ-ent color) represent links to other locations on the Web. They might be part of the same Web site or stored on another site elsewhere on the Internet. When you place the pointer over a link, it changes to a point-ing hand. Click a link (once) to follow it.

DILBERT ©1995 United Feature Syndicate, Inc.
Reprinted by permission of United Feature Syndicate, Inc.

4 When you're done exploring, select File ➤ Exit or click the Close button to quit the Internet Explorer. (Notice that the File menu maintains a list of the pages you've visited during this session.)

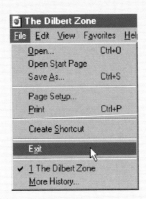

Cruising the Web with Internet Explorer

But you don't have to rely on preset links to specific addresses to launch your Web journeys. You can simply run the Internet Explorer (as long as you have a live Internet connection—MSN or otherwise).

1 Double-click the icon named *The Internet* on your Desktop.

▶ The Internet Explorer will start up (maximize the window if you haven't already), pointing to Microsoft Corporation's home page. If you need technical support or information about Microsoft, this is a dandy place to start. Otherwise, it's not too thrilling.

NOTE

The home page may change from time to time and quite likely won't match the screen shown here.

Going to a Specific Web Address

To head off for another location on the Web, you either need to follow an existing link, go to one of your favorite places in the Favorites menu (none, at first, until you add some), or enter an address manually. You can do this by selecting File ➤ Open Location and entering an address, but it will be easier to turn on the Address Bar and then enter addresses there whenever you like.

1 Select View ➤ Address Bar (unless it's already checked). Notice that you can also re-move the toolbar (don't) or the Status Bar (up to you).

2 Click in the Address Bar (the word *Address* will change to *Open*).

3 Type the address you want to go to (such as http://www.charm.net/ ~brooklyn/LitKicks.html).

NOTE

If you are copying an address from a publication, be careful to type it exactly as is, without any line breaks (even if the publisher was forced to break the lines to fit a design). Don't type a period or other punctuation at the end of the address (unless it's a /). If the address fails, try removing any hyphens that might have been added incorrectly. Many addresses have tildes in them (~) and often newspapers mess these up, placing them over characters or losing them entirely.

▶ You will be taken to the Web page whose address you entered.

4 Scroll through it if it's longer than one screen. Read it.

5 Follow any links you find interesting (place the pointer over the link and click once).

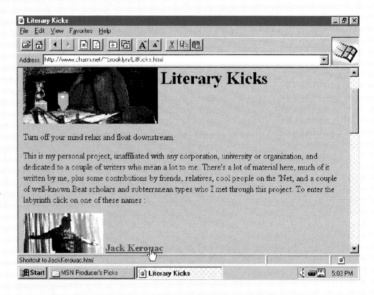

▶ It may take a moment for the new page to appear. Meanwhile, Internet Explorer will tell you what it's doing in the Status Bar.

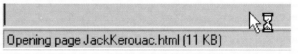

Retracing Your Steps

While the Web is great for following tangents and pursuing digressions, sometimes you'll overshoot what you're most interested in and you'll want to go back and read more at an earlier page, or pursue other tangents. Many Web pages incorporate their own links back to a *home page* and sometimes to other pages as well. Also, all Web browsers, including Internet Explorer, feature a Back command that takes you automatically to the previous page you visited (as well as a Forward command to re-retrace your steps).

1 After following a link, click the Back button in the toolbar. (The Home button takes you to Internet Explorer's home page—the Microsoft Corporation page until you change it.)

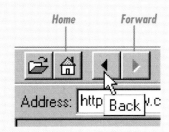

As you saw before, Internet Explorer also keeps a running list of pages visited on the bottom of the File menu.

2 Pull down the File menu and select a specific page to return to it. (The More History command will open up a folder with shortcuts to all the pages you've been to recently, not just during the current session.)

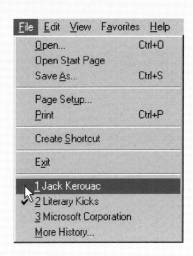

Customizing Internet Explorer

There are two things you might want to change about Internet Explorer. You might want to change the way pages are displayed, and you might want to change the default home page that comes up when you start the program. To change the home page, you first have to go to the page you want. If, in your Web browsing, you encounter a very useful starting point, with lots of links to subjects you're interested in, consider making that your home page. (One suggestion would be http://www.yahoo.com/, probably the most thorough table of contents on the Web.)

1 Select View ➤ Options.

▶ The Options dialog box appears.

2 Click the Appearance tab if it's not currently on top.

3 If you have a slow Internet connection and don't want pictures to automatically appear, uncheck *Show pictures.*

4 To change the default text and background colors (some pages will override your choices anyway), check *Use custom colors* and then click the two buttons to choose the colors you want.

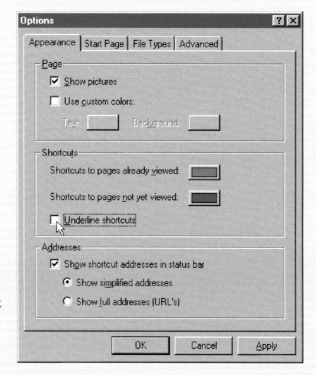

5 I recommend unchecking *Underline shortcuts.* Short-cuts are still easy to see but disrupt the flow of the words less when not underlined.

6 To change your home page, click the Start Page tab. (Internet Explorer calls it a Start Page but everyone else on the Web calls it a home page. Microsoft may be try-ing to differentiate this idea from that of a personal or corporate home page, which is a sort of storefront or front door on the Web.)

7 To make the current page your new home page, click Use Current.

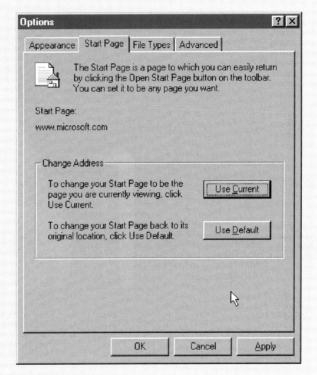

8 Click OK.

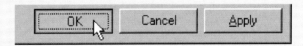

Adding a Web Page to Your Favorites

If you really like a page and want to visit it again, especially if it has more material in it than you can absorb in one sitting, you can add a shortcut to it in your Favorites menu. My advice is to err on the side of doing this whenever you think of it. You can always delete a shortcut, but you can't always find your way back to a fascinating Web site once you forget how you got there.

221

NOTE

If you do forget to make a shortcut and later on want to return to a Web page, try selecting File ➤ More History and see if there's still a shortcut to the page in question there.

If you've been exploring a Web site for a while, before adding it to your Favorites, think about returning to the main page, the home page (in that other sense), of the site you're visiting, unless you specifically want to add the subpage you've arrived at.

1 Select Favorites ➤ Add To Favorites.

▶ The Add To Favorites dialog box appears (yours may currently be empty).

2 Type a name for the shortcut (or use the supplied one).

3 Click the Add button.

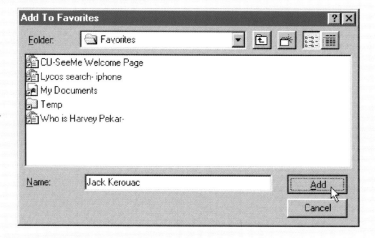

Creating a Shortcut to a Web Page

Another way to preserve a link to a place on the Web is to create a shortcut to it on your Desktop.

1 Select File ➤ Create Shortcut.

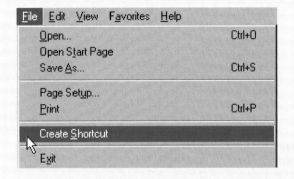

▶ Internet Explorer tells you it will create a shortcut to the current page on your Desktop.

2 Click OK.

NOTE

You can also save a complete copy of a Web document on your Desktop (or elsewhere) by selecting File ➤ Save As, typing a file name, and clicking Save.

---

3 Close the Internet Explorer by clicking the Close button.

▶ The shortcut you created will be there on the Desktop. You can double-click it to run Internet Explorer again and start at that particular page.

Jack Kerouac

Running Netscape or Other Web Browsers

If you've got the sort of connection required for Internet Explorer, then you can actually run *any* Windows Web browser over that same connection. This includes NCSA's Mosaic, other versions of Mosaic, EINET's WinWeb, InternetWorks, and Tiber, as well as Netscape Navigator, the most popular Windows browser. I'll use Netscape in the examples for the rest of this lesson. Some details of command names and functions will vary from browser to browser, but the gist will be the same.

Putting Your Browser on the Start Menu

If you've got another Web browser you like to use, such as Netscape, you should put it on the Start menu to make it easy to run, especially since any Web pages or shortcuts to them on your computer will automatically launch Internet Explorer once it's been installed. (If you want to change that, ask someone who knows how to change which programs .HTM files open with.)

> **NOTE**
> From now on I will refer explicitly to Netscape, but you should understand that you can substitute whichever your favorite browser might be.

Start by finding your copy of Netscape.

1 Select Start ➤ Find ➤ Files or Folders.

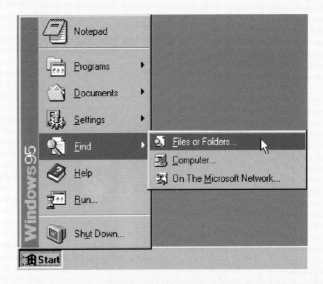

2 Type netscape.

3 Click the Find Now button.

4 When the program file is found, click the Stop button.

5 Scroll to (if necessary) and click the Netscape icon.

225

6 Drag it onto the Start button.

7 Close the Find dialog box.

Running a Web Browser

Now, just choose Netscape off the Start menu to run it.

1 Select Start ➤ Netscape.

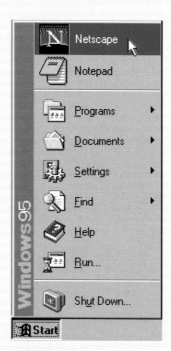

2 Maximize the Netscape window if it's not already maximized.

▶ You're taken to the Netscape home page (unless you've customized Netscape to start at another page automatically). If you're somewhere else, you can select Directory ➤ Netscape's Home to get to Netscape's home page.

Many browsers incorporate a What's New menu command or button to take you to a page containing some of the newest or most interesting recent additions to the Web. Sometimes you'll be taken to a choice of several listings.

3 Click the What's New! directory button (or select Directory ➤ What's New!).

Following Links

The essence of browsing the Web is following links to related and various other sites.

1 To follow a link, first move the pointer over the colored (usually blue, usually underlined) link text. The pointer will change to a pointing hand.

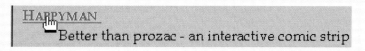

2 Then click (once). The link might flash as you click it.

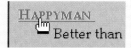

▶ You'll be taken to the place you chose—in this case, the home page of a comic strip called *HappyMan* that was linked from the Netscape What's New! page when I captured this shot (but is not there anymore). The address of the page can be seen in the Location box between the two sets of buttons.

3 To retrace your steps, click the Back button (in the top row of buttons).

By the way, if those multiple rows of buttons are taking up too much of your viewing space in Netscape, you can get rid of one (or both) of them. I recommend getting rid of the lower row, the Directory buttons, since they're all duplicated on the Directory menu.

4 Select Options ➤ Show Directory Buttons.

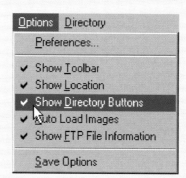

▶ On this menu, you can also turn off the toolbar and hide the Location box (I recommend keeping it up there).

Turning Off the Pictures

If your Internet connection is slow or you're mainly looking for written material, you can turn off the automatic loading of images.

1 Select Options ➤ Auto Load Images.

2 Type an address in the Location box (such as http://enterzone.berkeley.edu/enterzone.html, a magazine on the Web) and press Enter.

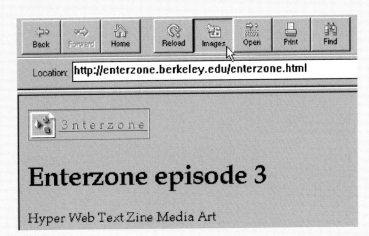

▶ As you arrive at the page, any art will be symbolized by a picture icon and the alternative text supplied with the art, if any, will appear as well (at least in a good Web browser). The page is displayed much more quickly this way than with art.

3 If you decide you *do* want to see the art on the current page, click the Images button on the toolbar.

▶ The art on that page will appear, replacing the dummy icons and alternative text.

Enterzone episode 3

Hyper Web Text Zine Media Art

E-Mailing a Web Document or Address

There are two ways to send mail around the Web. Some links are *mailto* links, and clicking them will bring up a mail window (or an associated mail program) with the To line filled in automatically. Most Web browsers also have a Mail Document command, with which you can send an address or entire Web page to anyone you want.

1 Select File ➤ Mail Document.

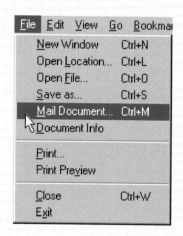

▶ A mail window will appear, with blanks for addressees, and a suggested Subject line consisting of the Web address you're mailing from.

2 Type an address to mail to (or your own address to save a copy of a document for later sending).

3 Click the Quote Document button to have the text of the Web page added to your e-mail message.

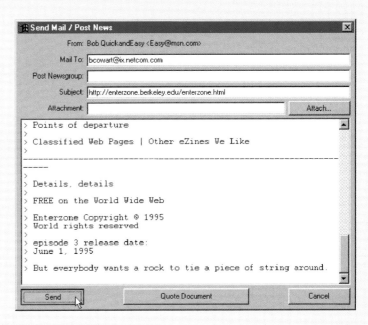

4 Type whatever message you like and click the Send button to mail the message.

Making a Bookmark (Adding to a Hotlist)

To save a location on the Web to return to later, just make a bookmark (some browsers call this adding to your hotlist).

1 Select Bookmarks ➤ Add Bookmark.

▶ The current page will appear at the bottom of the Bookmarks menu.

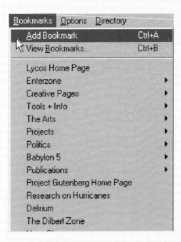

2 To reorganize the menu (or to see all the choices if there get to be too many to fit on the menu), select Bookmarks ➤ View Bookmarks.

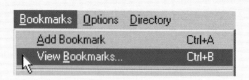

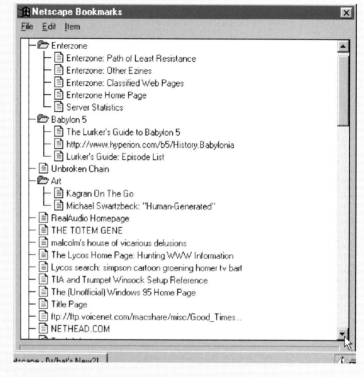

▶ The Netscape Bookmarks window will appear. To move a bookmark in the list, simply click it and drag it to a new location. To delete a bookmark, select it and press Delete, and then click Yes. You can also organize your bookmarks into folders and subfolders if that will help you keep track of them (use the commands on the Edit menu). Double-click a bookmark to move Netscape there.

3 When you're done with the Bookmarks window, click its Close button.

4 At other times, to go to a bookmark, pull down the Bookmarks menu and select the page you want to go to.

Exiting Netscape

When you've had your fun on the Web, you eventually have to quit.

1 Select File ➤ Exit.

▶ Netscape will close, waiting until the next time you feel like venturing from your Desktop onto the World Wide Web.

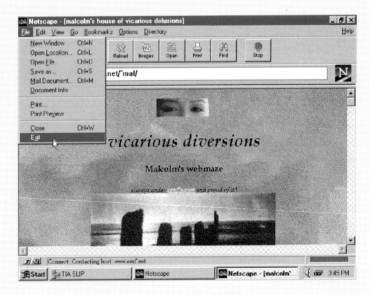

A Running Windows 95 for the First Time

If you (or, ideally, someone else) has just installed Windows 95 on your computer, and you're running it for the first time, you'll be taken through some steps just this once that you'll never have to deal with again.

You'll be asked some questions, but in just about every case, you'll just accept the suggested answer. If there's anything trickier to do, find a local guru to walk you through the steps.

Getting Ready to Start Windows for the First Time

Windows 95 will let you know that this is the first time you've run it on this particular computer, and you'll have to wait a little while for it to get all its ducks in a row.

Welcome to Windows

If there's ever been a version of Windows 95 installed on this computer in the past *and* that installation had different user profiles, each with their own password, then Windows will ask you to enter your username and password now. If not, not.

Setting Up Your Hardware

A dialog box will next appear, telling you "Windows 95 is now setting up your hardware and any Plug and Play devices you may have." Plug and Play devices are computer components or equipment that have been designed to work smoothly with Windows.

Setting Up Control Panel

Next, a dialog box will appear with a list of items for Windows to set up. A typical list would include

- Programs on Start Menu

- Windows Help

- MS-DOS Program Settings

- Time Zone

- Microsoft Exchange

but yours may differ. As Windows works its way through the list, each successive item will appear in boldface. When it gets to Time Zone, Windows will display a world map and you can make sure it's aimed at the time zone you live in. When it's correct, click OK.

After making it through the list, Windows will put up a dialog box telling you that you'll need to restart your computer for Windows' settings to take effect. Click OK.

Windows Tips

Your computer will restart and the Desktop will appear with such icons as are shown in Lesson 1. Also in the middle of the screen will appear the Welcome to Windows dialog box with a Windows tip.

Click the What's New button for a guide to the new features of Windows. Click the Online Registration button to register your copy of Windows with Microsoft electronically. If you do this, the Registration Wizard will collect hardware and software information from your hard disk and ask you for your name, address, and so on. If you don't do it, you should register Windows the traditional way, using the postcard enclosed with the package. (At work, someone may have already registered Windows for you).

When you've had enough of this dialog box, click Close. From now on, Windows will start up without all the preceding to-do.

B

Upgrading from Windows 3.1

If you've used earlier versions of Windows, particularly version 3.1, then you'll notice that a lot has changed. Most of the changes are for the better, I think you'll agree in the long run. (Many, if not all, of the changes to Windows specifically resolve problems or complaints that users had with the earlier versions.) Right now, though, everything is unfamiliar and might seem to be organized strangely.

This appendix will run down the major functional differences between Windows 95 and earlier verisons of Windows, to help ease your transition.

The Desktop Is Live

There was a Desktop in earlier versions of Windows, but it didn't really *do* anything. Mainly, it served as a holding pen for mininimized program windows.

Now, the Desktop is *live*, meaning that programs, documents, folders, and shortcuts can all stay there, indefinitely, in easy reach all of the time. This change means you'll have to think about the Desktop differently, not simply as the backdrop to your programs, but as your most readily accessible storage location.

> **NOTE**
> Programs written for older versions of Windows will usually run OK in Windows 95, but they won't recognize the Desktop for what it is. Instead, they'll see it as one of many folders inside the Windows folder.

See Part 4 for more about working on the Desktop.

No Program Manager, No File Manager

In earlier versions of Windows, most of the functions you might want to perform could be done through the Program Manager or the File Manager. The division of labor between these two programs was not always clear or easy to understand, but, for the most part, the File Manager illustrated the actual state of organization on your computer—the directory tree—and the Program Manager gave you access to an imaginary organizational layer of program groups.

In Windows 95, the Desktop has taken over the role formerly assigned to the File Manager, while (confusingly, to old-timers) somewhat resembling the Program Manager. The thing to remember is that the My Computer icon, along with the folder, programs, and documents to be found inside it, represents the actual organizational state of your computer. Lesson 16 explains how to browse the contents of your computer, starting with the My Computer icon.

> **NOTE**
> Windows does come with a program called Explorer that works very much the way the File Manager did, down to the split pane view showing folders on the left and folder contents on the right. See Lesson 25 if you're attached to this approach.

In a sense, the Programs submenu of the Start menu is the primary descendent of the Program Manager, because it gives you access to an organizational structure for your programs that does not depend on the actual state of the folders and files on your computer.

The Start Button and Menu

Speaking of which, the Start button and the menu it brings up are completely new, representing a breakthrough (at least for PC users) in the way to use the computer. The Start menu assembles the most useful commands and functions in one place, and allows you to create a hotlist of the programs you use most frequently.

Part 2 explains all about the Start button and how to add programs to the Start menu.

The Taskbar

The Taskbar replaces the old system of program icons being minimized onto the Desktop, and sometimes obscured by other windows. Now, every running program automatically gets a button on the Taskbar. The Taskbar is always visible (actually, you can go to great lengths to cover or hide it, as explained in Lesson 8, but even then it's easy to get to).

Part 2 explains all about the Taskbar.

Pop-Up Menus

Throughout Windows 95 and the programs written especially for it, you can move your mouse pointer to an object or area and click the right button to bring up a context-sensitive menu. Right-click on a document icon and you'll be able to copy it, make a shortcut from it, throw it away, send it to a floppy disk, and so on. Right-click on the Desktop and you can customize it. One way to explore Windows 95 is to try right-clicking on just about everything you see.

Pop-up menu shortcuts appear throughout the book but figure prominently in Lessons 17 through 21 in Part 4.

Shortcuts

Another completely new Windows 95 feature is shortcuts. Shortcuts are special icons that point to folders, programs, or documents elsewhere on your computer. Because they take up very little disk storage, you can sprinkle them freely—on your Desktop and in folders—so that it's always easy to get back to your work or to useful programs.

Lesson 20 explains how to create a shortcut (it's easy!).

All Icons Are Live

Whenever you see an icon, whether it be for a folder, a program, a document, or a shortcut, you can click on it, delete it, cut it, copy it, make a shortcut from it, or drag it to a new location. This includes the icons that appear inside Save and Open dialog boxes. You can always right-click icons to operate on them, and when you drag an icon, Windows either moves it, copies it, creates a shortcut from it, or tries to open it, depending on the destination. If you want to override the most obvious result, you can right-click and drag and then choose a result from the menu that pops up. Lessons 18 through 20 illustrate the "liveness" of icons in Windows.

Better Multitasking

Windows has supposedly always enabled you to do many things at once, but—as you probably know—the practical limitations were many. Often one process would hog all the attention of the computer and prevent you from doing something else. Other times, the computer would lag so badly that when it caught up to your actions, it would get confused and crash.

While it is still possible to overload or confuse your computer, depending on how much memory and other resources it has, it is now much easier to do many things at once and to have processes working in the background without messing up your other actions.

Great Find Command

In earlier versions of Windows, there was a Search command on the File Manager's File menu, but it could not search for text within documents, and it was slow and clumsy to use. Windows 95 has a very slick Find Files and Folders command on its Find menu that can search efficiently, look for text inside documents, find documents based on partial file names, and save search results. Lesson 22 shows you how to use it.

Long, Plain-English File Names

Finally, you can name your documents something beyond JQTRRPT1.SUM! Windows hides the file extensions as a matter of course, and lets you name documents anything you want (up to 255 characters) with spaces, capitalization, punctuation, you name it. Be careful when moving documents to and from computers running older versions of Windows, though, because files all still have an old-style name of the eight-character-dot-three-character kind, and long names can get lost in the transition.

239

See for Yourself

That about sums up the differences between the newest version of Windows and older ones. The quickest way to get comfortable with the changes is to jump right in and start using Windows 95.

Index

Throughout this index, **boldfaced** page numbers indicate primary discussions of a topic. *Italicized* page numbers indicate illustrations.

H

hard drives
    displaying contents of, **162–163**,
        162–163
    icons for, *7*
    mapping, **179–181**
    opening, **101–102**
hardware, setting up, 234
help
    closing, **65**
    for dialog boxes, **64–65**
    for Microsoft Network, **211–212**
    on Start menu, **62**
    topic selection for, **63–64**
Help button for e-mail, *171*
Help command, *62*
Help option, 23
Help Topics button, *64*
Help Topics: Windows Help dialog
    box, *63*, 65
hidden documents, displaying, 108
Hide files of these types: option, 109
Hide MS-DOS file extensions
    option, 108–109, *108*
hiding
    Taskbar, **51–52**
    windows, **12–13**
Home button on Internet Explorer,
    219
home pages on Web, 217–219, 221
hot icons, *81*, **238–239**

I

icons
    arranging, **100–101**, **137–140**,
        143–144
    copying, 42, **113–117**, **119–121**
    detail view for, **104–105**, *105*
    hot, *81*, **238–239**
    large, 108
    moving, **39**, **117–118**, 120–121,
        141–142
    printing from, **88–89**
    small, **103–104**, 109

Images button, *229*
Inbox folder
    for e-mail, 170–171, *170*
    for Microsoft Network, *198*
Inbox icon, *4*, *5*, *168*
Index tab, 63
Internet, **208–210**, *208*. *See also* Web
Internet Center icon, *208*
Internet Center window, 208–209,
    208
Internet Explorer
    cruising with, **216–219**
    customizing, **219–221**, *220–221*
    starting, **214–216**
Internet icon, *216*
InternetWorks browser, 224

J

Join Now button, *192*
joining
    chat rooms, **206–207**
    Microsoft Network, **192–194**,
        193–194

L

large icons, 108
Large Icons command, 108
Line up Icons command, *137*
links on Web, following, **227–228**
List command, 104
listing folder contents, **162–163**,
    162–163
live Desktop, 236
live icons, *81*, **238–239**
loading Web pictures, turning off,
    229–230
Look in list box, 178

M

mail
    Exchange for, **168–171**, *169*, 174
    on Microsoft Network, **197–199**
    reading messages in, **171**, *171*
    replying to messages in, **172**, *172*

    sending messages in, **173–174**,
        173
    with Web browsers, **230–231**, *231*
Mail Document command, *230*
mail window, *231*
mailto links with Web browsers, 230
Map Network Drive command, *180*
Map Network Drive dialog box, *180*
mapping network drives, **179–181**
Maximize button, *7*, *15*
maximizing windows, **15–16**
Member Assistance bar, *211*
Member Assistance window, *212*
Member ID for Microsoft Network,
    194, 195
menu bars, *7*
menus
    pop-up, 238
    from right-clicking, *7*
messages
    on BBSs on Microsoft Network,
        204–205, *204–205*
    mail. *See* mail
    newsgroup, **210**
Microsoft Exchange
    for e-mail, **168–171**, *169*, 174
    exiting, 174
    for Microsoft Network, **198–199**
Microsoft Network (MSN)
    BBSs on, **202–206**, *204*
    categories on, **200–201**, *200–202*
    chat rooms on, **206–208**, *207*
    contents of, **189–190**, *189*
    Favorite Places on, **206**, 208,
        210–211, *211*
    help for, **211–212**
    for Internet access, **208–210**, *208*
    joining, **192–194**, *193–194*
    mail on, **197–199**
    payment method for, *191*
    pricing information for, *190*
    rules for, **192**, *192*
    signing in to, **195–197**, *195*
    signing out of, **212–213**, *213*
    signing-up for, **186–189**,
        187–189